JEWISH-CHRISTIAN DIALOGUE

One Woman's Experience

MARY C. BOYS

Mary C. Boys

1997 Madeleva Lecture
in Spirituality

PAULIST PRESS
New York/Mahwah, N.J.

To Sara S. Lee
Cherished Friend and Beloved Colleague
BeKavod

The Publisher gratefully acknowledges use of excerpts from the following copy-righted works: From "When a Christian Chants the Qur'an" by George Dardess (*Commonweal* 122/1; January 13, 1995). Copyright 1995 by the Commonweal Foundation. Reprinted by permission of the Commonweal Foundation. From *Encountering God* by Diana Eck. Copyright 1993 by Diana Eck. Reprinted by permission of Beacon Press. From *The Jew in the Lotus* by Rodger Kamenetz. Copyright 1994 by Rodger Kamenetz. Reprinted by permission of HarperCollins Publishers, Inc. From *Available Light* by Marge Piercy. Copyright 1988 by Middlemarsh Inc. Reprinted by permission of Alfred A. Knopf Inc.

Cover design by Moe Berman.

Boys, Mary C.
Jewish–Christian Dialogue: One Woman's Experience / by Mary C. Boys.
     p.   cm. — (Madeleva lecture in spirituality : 1997)
    Includes bibliographical references.
    ISBN 0-8091-3738-0 (alk. paper)
    1. Christianity and other religions. 2. Catholic Church—Relations. 3. Commitment (Psychology)—Religious aspects—Christianity. 4. Religious pluralism—Christianity. 5. Spiritual formation—Catholic Church. 6. Religious pluralism—Catholic Church. I. Title. II. Series.
BR127.B65 1997
261.2–dc21
                        96–40261
                        CIP

Published by Paulist Press
997 Macarthur Boulevard
Mahwah, New Jersey 07430

Printed and bound in the
United States of America

CONTENTS

iii

ACKNOWLEDGMENTS

I am grateful to Professor Keith J. Egan and Sister Rose Ann Schultz, C.S.C., of the Center for Spirituality at Saint Mary's College for the invitation to be 1997 Madeleva Lecturer in Spirituality. My thanks also to Drs. Dorothy C. Bass and Katherine Kurs for their close reading of the manuscript and encouragement to pursue this topic. The dedication expresses my profound gratitude for the privilege of working with Sara S. Lee, director of the Rhea Hirsch School of Education at Hebrew Union College–Jewish Institute of Religion, Los Angeles. Our collaboration is not only professionally enriching but a personal joy.

Mary C. Boys, S.N.J.M., holds a master's and doctorate from Columbia University and is the Skinner and McAlpin Professor of Practical Theology at Union Theological Seminary in New York City. She is the author of *Biblical Interpretation in Religious Education* (Birmingham: Religious Education Press, 1980), more than *Educating in Faith: Maps and Visions* (San Francisco: Harper & Row, 1989), and fifty articles and chapters. Former president of the Association of Professors and Researchers in Religious Education, she is a member of the Christian Scholars Group on Jews and Judaism, the Abrahamic Accord, and an advisor to the Valparaiso Project on the Education and Formation of People in Faith. She is a member of the Sisters of the Holy Names of Jesus and Mary.

1. INTRODUCTION

The Madeleva Lecture honors a woman of adventurous spirit who offered educational leadership at a critical point in U.S. Catholicism. This occasion reflects our esteem for a scholar who completed a Ph.D. in medieval literature at the University of California at Berkeley in 1925 while commuting three hours each way to a high school where she served as principal, head of the English department, and teacher of English and French— and whose dissertation appeared in print soon thereafter. Who among us cannot be edified by the talent and energy of Sister Madeleva (1887–1964), who founded one college (Saint Mary's-of-the-Wasatch in Salt Lake City in 1926) and served with distinction as president of another for more than a quarter of a century, all the while continuing to publish poetry, including some so passionate it made her religious superiors nervous. Under her leadership, Saint Mary's College opened the School of Sacred Theology in the summer of 1943, thereby making it possible for nuns and other laity to earn master's and doctoral degrees in theology. She likewise offered her leadership about five years later to the Sister Formation Movement, which stimulated the higher education of women in religious congregations.[1]

It seems right and just that a lecture celebrating the pioneering and visionary spirit of Sister Madeleva should focus on a topic that requires breaking with conventional thinking, evokes the poet's disciplined passion, and necessitates imagining new structures. Thus, I propose we invoke her intrepid spirit as we explore the argument that serious and sustained encounter with another religious tradition is imperative for developing a healthy commitment as a Christian in a pluralistic world.

I will preface this argument with remarks about the way it fits into the flow of topics in the Madeleva lectures. Then in the first major section, I will offer some reflections about the nature of religious commitment needed in our time. In the second part, I will tell five stories that portray serious and sustained encounters across religious boundaries. I believe these cases illustrate the most significant elements of the religious commitment I've outlined in the first section. In part three, I will speak specifically and personally about the ways in which I understand the encounter with Jews and Judaism to be transformative of Christian life on both the level of practice and theological understanding. I will also suggest a few implications for educating and forming Christians in light of the interreligious encounters I have described.

The twelve previous Madeleva lectures by Catholic women scholars examine issues in which women's experience and perspectives are vital. They have ranged from exhortations regarding women's contribution to a troubled world to illustrations of how women gifted with the religious imagination might breathe new life into the public prayer of the church, including a reflection on passion in the lives of medieval mystics Hildegard of Bingen and Hadewijch of Antwerp. The lecturers have dealt with a series of "women and _____": the Word, teaching, power, creativity, sexuality, ecology, with the most recent lectures focusing on the experiences of African American and Hispanic women, respectively. It's an impressive mosaic.

It may appear that my argument bears little relation to the particularities of women's experience and perspectives. On one level this is true. Though I am a feminist informed by feminist and womanist theological and educational works, I find these sources provide me with relatively little

3

material to draw upon explicitly in developing my argument. Moreover, I believe it is unwise to argue that women *qua women* have a unique contribution to make to religious pluralism, just as we are discovering the superficiality of earlier feminist claims that women are *by nature* more caring, more able to develop and sustain relationships, and so on.

On the other hand, the potential of interreligious encounter for enriching religious commitment is integrally connected to the topics taken up by previous lecturers. Let two examples suffice here. They both involve a sort of hermeneutic of suspicion: Why are women so often missing from the picture when interreligious exchange goes on at various formal levels? Think of the gathering of the world's religious leaders at Assisi in 1986 for the World Day of Prayer for peace with its virtually all-male cast of characters! Similarly, in Catholicism a women's expertise in ecumenism and interreligious affairs is too often confined to an occasional theological committee. When it comes to the official level (e.g., the Commission on Religious Relations with Jews), male clerics are once again at the center of the picture. So issues of power, as Joan Chittister explored in 1990, are pertinent.

On a more positive note, one of the stories I will tell in part two, the dramatic reversal in the self-understanding of the Sisters of Sion, testifies eloquently to the willingness of women in the church to confront their parochialism and to take risks in order to honor a new vision. Moreover, insofar as women have been socialized to attend to the relational and to take care of details of hospitality, they bring invaluable skills to the interreligious forum.

2. RELIGIOUS COMMITMENT

My own work, in a phrase, involves *educating for* religious commitment, primarily but not exclusively within the Christian community (and especially in my home tradition of Catholicism). I hunger to learn more about the dynamics that shape commitments, to understand what factors influence persons to live with integrity. Our world, I believe, desperately needs religiously committed men and women—persons for whom care of the widow and the orphan take precedence over accumulation of material goods and ego striving, persons who reject violence and work for peace. Such commitments are vital everywhere, but especially in a democracy where, as legal scholar Stephen Carter has pointed out, religions can serve two vital functions: (1) as sources of moral understanding preventing a majoritarian system from deteriorating into simple tyranny and (2) as a forum mediating between the citizen and the apparatus of government, thereby offering an independent moral voice. Religion, because it mobilizes passion rather than merely appealing to reason, is a potent force for good in a society too often under the sway of principalities and powers.[2]

Precisely because religion mobilizes passion, however, it is always susceptible to fanaticism. Tragically, religious commitments can be pathological, as both the daily paper and history provide ample evidence. We have only to bring to mind, for example, oxymorons like "Christian hate groups" or "Christian supremacists," which illustrate all too vividly the possibility of religious commitments mutating into zealotry, bigotry, fascism and violence—what David Tracy calls the "appalling litany of murders, inquisitions, holy wars, obscurantisms, and exclusivisms."[3]

So we need to be clear what sort of religious commitment we desire. I believe we need to educate for religious commitments that are both clear *and* ambiguous, rooted *and* adaptive. We might call this an *education for paradox,* as it asks us to dwell in a dynamic tension.[4]

One pole of the paradox is more familiar, as it is often posed as an ideal by church leaders: educating persons who are knowledgeable about their faith and grounded in its traditions and practices in such a way that their religious identity is manifest in the way they live. Indeed, who among us could not hope for such an ideal? Would not Christians live with greater vitality and responsibility if more of us grappled with the radical call of Jesus? What if Christians were to model ourselves on the decisive dispositions of Jesus, such as his surrender to God, gratitude, readiness for service and self-sacrificing love, and preferential option for the poor? What if we were to take up in our own way the paradigmatic actions in the life of Jesus, such as the cross, foot washing, prayer, outreach to those who were excluded or marginal, healing, forgiveness, love of enemies, and nonviolence? What if we were to enter imaginatively into his utopian teaching about God's reign?[5] Would not Christians have a more profound message to bring to the public square if we could interpret biblical texts in their literary and historical contexts rather than assemble proof texts? Would not Catholics be more of a leaven in society if we were steeped in the sacramental imagination?

Let me be clear. The challenge to educate persons who are so immersed in their religious tradition that they can be a transforming presence in the world is enormous. It is not just nostalgia for "old-time religion" that gives us pause about the rootlessness of the "generation of seekers."[6] We have genuine cause for concern.

The other pole of the paradox may be even more difficult to deal with, but it is no less important if religious commitment is to be healthy: teaching about our traditions of faith in ways that give religious commitments dimensions of ambiguity and adaptability. On the face of it, it may seem that ambiguous and adaptable commitments are anomalous—or at least threatening to the stability of a tradition. To the contrary.

Ambiguity, from the Latin *ambigere,* to drive both ways, suggests that we need to resist what educational theorist Stephen Brookfield terms "premature absolutes," lest we close off the mystery of religious experience and confuse the poetry of religious language with the prosaic renderings of propositions.[7] Allowing for ambiguity in our commitments enables us to admit doubt and to acknowledge the disequilibrium that wrests us from smugness and throws us upon the God who is both hidden and revealed, utterly simple and infinitely complex—and always surprising.

Adaptability stems from rootedness, from foundations that allow for movement, just as the tree with deep roots can survive a violent storm and a building engineered with the proper degree of oscillation can withstand an earthquake. Failure to adapt can be destructive, or may distort a tradition or institution. Boston's Isabella Stewart Gardner Museum offers a vivid illustration of the latter. A recreation of a fifteenth-century Venetian palazzo built between 1899 and 1901, the museum houses Gardner's eclectic collection of furnishings, paintings, textiles, and sculpture. Under the conditions of her will, all items must be displayed intact in perpetuity; neither rearrangement nor addition is permitted. So at certain times of the day, items must be covered up, lest they be damaged by sunlight. What has been called the "greatest art theft ever"—a robbery in 1990 in which twelve artworks worth an estimated $300 million were taken—adds another surreal note. Where great works such as Vermeer's "The Concert" or Rembrandt's "The Storm on the Sea of Galilee" once hung, a visitor now finds simply a blank wall, to which a small sign is attached, "Stolen on March 18, 1990."[8]

Presumably, Isabella Stewart Gardner thought that the terms specified in her will insured the stability of her collection. Ironically, however, by preventing the museum staff from adapting to conditions, she jeopardized the ultimate longevity of the collection of her treasures.

So, too, in the life of faith. Simply repeating formulae from era to era does not insure that their meaning will remain unchanged.

Thus, my conviction: we need religious commitments that are clear *and* ambiguous, rooted *and* adaptive. But as an educator, I am always faced with "how?"

That is a big question, one that will take a lifetime to answer. No one method or emphasis will accomplish this. *Nevertheless, I am convinced that serious and sustained encounter with another religious tradition is one of most significant factors in forming religious commitments that are simultaneously clear*

10

and ambiguous, rooted and adaptive. The "serious and sustained" encounter, moreover, not only has potential for enabling us to live more intelligently and sensitively in a pluralistic world, but also stimulates us to a more vital understanding and practice of our particular tradition of faith.

Rather than arguing this on the level of abstraction, let us turn now to five stories in order to give texture to the argument.

3. INTERRELIGIOUS ENCOUNTER: FIVE STORIES

In October 1990 a small delegation of Jews from the United States traveled to a remote Indian town in the foothills of the Himalayas, Dharamsala, to meet with the fourteenth Dalai Lama at the latter's request. As the leader of 115,000 Tibetan refugees living in exile in India since 1959, the Dalai Lama hoped to learn from Jews how to survive as a people. China's occupation of Tibet, begun in 1950 and intensified after 1959, has devastated Tibetan Buddhism. An estimated 1.2 million Tibetans have died, public teaching of Buddhism has been proscribed, more than 6,000 monasteries have been destroyed, and many monks and nuns persecuted. Thus the Dalai Lama's poignant request to Jews, "Tell me your secret, the secret of Jewish spiritual survival in exile."[9]

For Rabbi Irving "Yitz" Greenberg, teaching Jewish history to the Dalai Lama was an act of love: "All of us came here with a sense of wanting to learn from you, but also with a feeling of love. The love is identification, for we have suffered some of the tragedies you have suffered, and we would like to help in some way." Jews have, as Rodger Kamenetz observes in his splendid account of the journey, "a rich menu of crises to choose from" in reflecting on survival.[10]

So Greenberg focused his presentation for the Dalai Lama on Jewish survival in the wake of the destruction of Jerusalem in 70 C.E. That devastation—including the loss of the Temple and priesthood, famine, and expulsion from Jerusalem—raised profound questions among Jews about why God did not intervene to save them from Roman destruction. Greenberg's reading is that the rabbis exercised brilliant leadership in interpreting the destruction to mean that God "was becoming less visible, more hidden....manifest divine activity was being curtailed."[11] They concluded that God's mighty deeds of power—parting the seas and providing them with manna—had sustained the people in the past, but that, after the destruction of 70 C.E., Jews had to take a more active role in the covenant. "Divine Presence was becoming more hidden so that the Jewish people could become true partners with God."[12] Downplaying messianic and mystical intervention, the rabbis thus emphasized Torah and its interpretation through the melange of law and story known as the Talmud. So Jewish texts became a "portable homeland," and it became incumbent upon each Jew to become learned in order that every aspect of life might be suffused with Jewish values and meanings.

Greenberg explained to the Dalai Lama how rituals and customs nurtured remembrance. For example, on *Tisha b'Av* (the ninth of Av), which commemorates the Babylonian destruction of the Temple in 586 B.C.E. as well as the Roman destruction in 70 C.E., Jews retell and reenact the destruction and loss of Jerusalem. They gather in other losses to the observance on the ninth of Av: the fall of Judea to the Romans in the wake of the Bar-Kokhba revolt in 135 C.E., the burning of the Talmud in Paris in 1242, the expulsion of the Jews from England in 1290 and from Spain in 1492, and the beginning of the deportation from the Warsaw ghetto to Treblinka. Following a three-week period of preparation, on *Tisha b'Av* Jews act out rituals of mourning. They read the Book of Lamentations in semidarkness in the evening service in the synagogue. Fasting from food and drink for a full twenty-four hours, refraining from washing or wearing leather shoes or perfume, and giving up sexual relations, Jews are "unshaven, unwashed, hungry, people [who] reexperience the tragedy of the Destruction."[13]

Other rituals and customs, of course, memorialize more joyous events in rich, sensory ways. Shabbat observances anticipate the messianic redemption, and those of the Passover celebrate redemption. The key, as Greenberg stresses, is that preserving the tradition required the rabbinic sages to find the "courage to renew."[14]

Such instruction impressed the Dalai Lama: "The points you have mentioned really strike at the heart of how to sustain one's culture and tradition. This is what I call the Jewish secret—to keep your tradition. In every important aspect of human life, there is something to remind. We have to return, we have to return, we have to return, to take responsibility."[15]

This Jewish-Buddhist encounter, however, included more than passing on the "secret" of Jewish survival. It also involved deep conversation about mysticism, at times to the discomfort of some of the Jewish delegates who prized more rational ways of thought and practice. When several of the Jewish delegates expounded upon their esoteric texts, making connections between *kabbalah* (mystical tradition) and Buddhist *tantra* (advanced meditation teachings), the Dalai Lama seemed fascinated. They exchanged specifics of their respective meditation practices, discovering both similarities and differences. Noting the reserve of other Jewish delegates about mysticism, the Dalai Lama offered them advice: if such teachings are largely inaccessible to Jews, they must resolve to "open the doors and open them wide."[16]

The days in Dharamsala were not without their tensions. Having encountered in Buddhists a community that abhorred anger, the Jewish delegates were both impressed and skeptical. On the one hand desirous of learning from them how to deal with conflict in a more creative and nonviolent way, and on the other, dubious that anger could be overcome, the Jews questioned Buddhist explanations for evil. When a monk explains that the Holocaust was the "result of past karma," Kamenetz reports that he is "shocked, a little outraged." But when the Dalai Lama expands upon Buddhism's attitude toward the enemy ("[T]he so-called enemy, or the external factor, is something secondary. The main force is one's own, either in the collective karma or individual karma"), Kamenetz sees a way of overcoming a sense of despair and hopelessness. He notes that, though Jews have always felt strongly about righting wrongs, whatever the cost, they may not have taken sufficient account of the toll anger takes:

Anger over the Holocaust has paralyzed many Jews spiritually and emotionally....On the other hand, especially after seeing the real conflict in the Tibetan exile community over how to handle the Chinese, I wasn't so sure that the Dalai Lama's position was...realistic....Is Jewish anger, however damaging in some respects, essential to Jewish survival? Or will a Judaism that continues, in some ways, to dwell on and even nourish a sense of anger over past injustices prove to be an increasingly burdensome heritage to pass on to our children as we enter the twenty-first century?[17]

Another tension touched a raw nerve. Proportionally, a high number of Jews have become practitioners of Buddhism, and with fewer than 5 percent of American Jews defining themselves religiously, "JUBUs"—Jewish-Buddhists—"represent an abnormally large percentage of a precious pool of energetic, talented, and spiritually committed Jews."[18] Many of those who had been drawn to Buddhism had found Jewish mystical experience inaccessible. Verifying this, Rabbi Jonathan Omer-Man, one of those who had taught the Dalai Lama about Jewish esoteric teachings, remarked, "There are more Jews seeking the esoteric in Dharamsala than there are in my synagogue in Los Angeles."[19] They had found a spiritual wealth in Buddhism that they had not in Judaism—a source of consternation and sadness to the Jewish delegates.

For poet and professor of English Rodger Kamenetz, the encounter with Tibetan Buddhism revealed new dimensions of Judaism. The profound discussion with the monks, and the Dalai Lama in particular, had unleashed a new energy among the Jewish participants as they discussed and davened (prayed) with deepened intensity:

"The irony is, I had to travel halfway around the world to Dharamsala to discover the utility of Jewish prayer. Our davening brought us together and changed the environment around us, transforming Kashmir Cottage, a Buddhist guest house, into Beth Kangra, the open-air synagogue of the Himalayas."[20]

Kamenetz notes another outcome of his experience of Buddhist India: "If only Jews could see themselves as sweetly as the Dalai Lama saw us. Then we would see Judaism renewed."[21]

A CHRISTIAN-ISLAMIC ENCOUNTER

George Dardess, a Roman Catholic who teaches English in upstate New York, sought to overcome his ignorance of Islam by studying Arabic and then the Qur'an.[22] He grew close to his Arabic teacher, Dr. Muhmmad Shafiq, imam of Rochester's Islamic Center. Dardess learned not only to read the text of the Qur'an but to chant it, taking lessons in Qur'anic *tajwid*. (The word *Qur'an* means "recitation," and the text is meant to be heard aloud.) Chanting furthered his appreciation of Islam: "My understanding is that being Muslim means just this, allowing the voice of the Qur'an, God's voice, to penetrate one's heart, with the result that one's behavior radically changes."[23]

18

Dardess' study had transformed what had earlier been superficial and distorted knowledge of Islam gained from the media. He began to see the profundity of Islam. But had his experience of the Qur'an changed him in any way? Had he, in becoming more of a Muslim, thereby become less of a Christian? Or had his immersion in Islam enabled him to become more of a Christian—and, if so, in what ways?

Dardess is convinced that he had become "more joyfully and wonderingly a Christian than before," primarily because "the Qur'an has enlarged my sense of the Word of God." Having known Jesus as the "Word made flesh," the creative power of the Father, Dardess learned attentiveness to the Word:

> The Word of God in the Qur'an is not transformative in the same way or to the same degree [as Christians understand Christ's saving actions to be]. Islam vigorously denies that human nature has fallen so low as to require God's salvific action....What the Qur'an "adds" for me—though, for God, there can be no question of a deficiency, of an adding or a subtracting—is a reinvigorated emphasis on the voice as the agent of embodiment....A prayerful recitation of the Qur'an, which requires that key ingredient of Muslim worship, *taqwa,* or absolute

attentiveness to God's "signs," primarily to those given in the Qur'an itself, has led me to a more prayerful attention to the Christian Word at Mass and in private Bible reading. Word presence is real presence. The force of this truth, acknowledged by me before, but often lukewarmly, has been quickened by my Qur'anic chanting.[24]

But, Dardess presses further, can the Qur'an's voice exceed merely invigorating his dulled consciousness of the power of the spoken Word? Is there danger here, a point beyond which engagement with Qur'anic texts imperils his love of the risen Christ? If, Dardess asks, most Christians, including himself, believe that there can be no salvation except through Christ, how can he chant the Qur'an sincerely without assuming that it has the same revelatory power as the Gospels?

But Dardess also realizes that his attachment to the Christ cannot be reduced to a series of dogmatic declarations.

[T]he risen Christ is present to me, not only at Mass, but at every beat of my heart, in every circumstance. There is no limit to this penetration. Similarly with everyone else, including those who do not know him as risen Lord, or who do not know him at all. Yet my belief in his universality does not entitle me to make claims of superior knowledge. I could never confront Dr. Shafiq with the statement that, whatever he may think to the contrary, Jesus is with him. Not good manners but humility prohibits my doing so....As I stand before the cross chanting the Qur'an, I do not find myself, God's creature, moved to argue about discrepancies, even ones as significant as those involving Jesus' true nature or importance. My conviction that the language of the Qur'an is also God's language overrides what would otherwise bring me to disagree with it as a mere human utterance. In such moments of enthusiasm—and they come often—I find nothing to hinder me from making the Muslim *shahada,* the credal statement of faith in one God and in Muhammad as his prophet.[25]

Dardess grew so close to his teacher that Dr. Shafiq invited him to join the prayer line with the other men at *salat,* the prayer performed daily at five prescribed times. Shafiq told him that he saw him as a Muslim in the truest sense, that is, that Dardess believed in the one God; yet Shafiq never sought to convert him, following the Qur'anic text "let there be no compulsion in religion." Honored by Shafiq's invitation, Dardess is also conflicted by it. Participating in *salat* seemed to him rather like an outsider to Christianity partaking of

21

Communion. Despite his regard for and trust in Dr. Shafiq, Dardess confesses that he feels a restraint about joining the prayer line; it seems a form of trespass. His reserve is based neither on a fear of what fellow Catholics might say, nor of what Muslims less enlightened than Dr. Shafiq might think to find him, a Christian, at their side during *salat*. Rather, says Dardess, "it's that the communal action of prayer, as opposed to the more private version of it represented by chanting the Qur'an, assumes a full commitment to those with whom one prays. By 'full commitment'…[I mean] primarily a desire to make one's religion one's home. In marital terms, it means monogamy."[26]

Dardess described to Dr. Shafiq his reluctance to take part in *salat* as a form of fasting analogous to the "fast" when, as a catechumen, he awaited baptism and confirmation as a Catholic Christian. During the catechumenate, he had felt a sharp hunger for the Eucharist, but also a "joy for the hunger itself, as if it were important in God's plan that I experience fully the hunger before I knew its satisfaction." In restraining himself from performing *salat*, he was putting himself "in the position of knowing fully the extent and meaning of my desire."[27]

Unlike his experience in the catechumenate, Dardess may never end his "fast" from *salat*. But he realizes that antiquated categories have been broken, that an old wineskin has begun to split. His desire? "May all Christians know the complex delight granted me to know our God at the boundary of our practice and understanding."[28]

Diana Eck, a Christian scholar of comparative religions who teaches at Harvard University, offers eloquent testimony to the "complex delight" granted to those who know God at the boundary of practice and understanding. In her recent book *Encountering God,* Eck traces her journey from her Bozeman, Montana, home to her life in India as a student of its multiple religious traditions, particularly Hinduism.[29] Nurtured in Methodism in her youth, she discovers new depths of Christianity through her involvement in the religious life of South Asia. Having experienced in the give-and-take of dialogue the truth of Indian philosopher Krishnamurti's claim that "relationship is the mirror in which we see ourselves as we really are," Eck writes, "My encounter with Hindus has enabled me to understand my own faith more clearly and has required that I understand my own faith differently. It would only be honest to say that my faith as a Christian has been shaped by several religious traditions."[30]

I suggest we might find in her work two

important and interconnected themes: a widening of theological horizons and a deepening of spirituality. As an introductory note, I would like to underscore her affirmation that her serious and sustained encounter with India's religious tradition *enabled* her to understand her home tradition *more clearly* even as it *required* her to understand it *differently.* In Eck's case, it is transparent that such an encounter forms religious commitments that are *clear and ambiguous, rooted and adaptive.*

As a comparativist, Eck inquires into what Muslims, Hindus, or Buddhists mean when they speak of Allah, Vishnu, or the Buddha. But in Eck's life, the more distant stance of the scholar ultimately gives way to the existential quest for what their understandings might mean *for her as a Christian.* In what ways has her immersion in Hinduism, with its "articulate philosophical theism" and its "astonishing, vivid, multi-armed and multi-headed gods" enlarged her theological horizons?[31]

In a word, it becomes evident that Eck's sojourns in India have fostered awe before the complexity and mystery of God. Hinduism offers theological strategies that help Western monotheists to think more deeply about the infinite God who reveals through many names and forms. To enter into Hindu conceptions of "oneness" and "manyness" is to find language that both stretches our images of the divine and offers analogies to our conceptions of the Triune God. Experience in Hindu life has led Eck to a new appreciation that "all the great monotheisms, however unitary they may seem from a distance, become more complex the closer we get....The one we call God is both beyond the reach of the human imagination and at the same time present in very tangible, seemingly mundane, and human ways."[32]

For instance, Eck tells of an evening spent at a temple in a town in southern India, Trivandrum, in which an eighteen-foot granite image of Vishnu resting upon the coils of a serpent named Endless occupies the center of the inner sanctum. Walking the temple's concentric corridors en route to the sanctum, Eck remembers Psalm 27: "One thing I have asked of the LORD, that will I seek after; to live in the house of the LORD all the days of my life, to behold the beauty of the LORD, and to inquire in his temple" (v. 4). She joins a crowd of other women at the time for the evening offering of oil lamps. With drums beating and bells ringing to a crescendo, an attendant flings open the central pair of doors to reveal part of the immense image of Vishnu. Next a pair of doors to the left were opened, showing the upper portion of Vishnu, then the doors to the right, revealing his feet. Though in the press of the crowd Eck could not see the image well, she writes that as the many lamps were waved in honor of Vishnu, she "could see the suggestion of his presence there. It was a sense of enormous presence, dimly seen, illumined for a moment by oil lamps and by the intermediary grace of the priest who moved the soft light before the long body of the Lord." The worshipers held their lamps high toward Vishnu's face, then to his feet. After the last lamp was presented to Vishnu, it was given to the people as a blessing. "Four hundred pairs of hands stretched out to touch the flame and then touch its blessing to the forehead. Mine were among them."[33]

Eck reflects:

Seeing that triptych in the temple in Trivandrum, with its three glimpses of a God larger than one could fully comprehend, was a moment of recognition for me, and the experience of God's presence there was describable only as worship. My experience as a Christian was surely different from that of the Hindus pressed against me on either side. But we shared the sense of delight and revelation as the doors were opened, and perhaps some sense of both the majesty and mystery of the Divine. I thought of nothing at the time. It was a moment of total presence, not of reflection. But as I left the temple, looking frequently back through door upon door, light and shadow, in the direction of Vishnu resting upon the serpent called Endless, I began thinking about what we Christians call the Trinity, the threefold vision of God as creator, redeemer, and spirit. I could not get it out of my mind—this triple yet singular revelation of the one God, the glimpses we had through the doors that were opened upon his presence, the over-whelming sense that no vantage point could enable us to see the whole.[34]

Moreover, Eck believes it is precisely her Christian faith that enables her to acknowledge God's presence in a Hindu temple or in the life of a Hindu; her encounter with God, Christ, and the Spirit enables her to have a sense of what God's presence is like. She adds, "I would even say that it is Christ who enables Christians—in fact, chal-lenges us—to recognize God especially where we don't expect to do so and where it is not easy to do so."[35]

India's theological gift to Eck is the discovery that "God can be addressed as Mother, can wear the ashes of the cremation pyre, or can beckon us to dance." But then it should not be surprising that one might recognize the God of Abraham and Sarah in Trivandrum or Banaras "if God is indeed the One we say God is—the creator of heaven and earth and all that is therein."[36]

India is likewise a place where she has learned new dimensions of the incarnation. The "five faces of Shiva" and the many *rasas* or "tastes" of Krishna, expressive of the complexity of God's presence in Hinduism, provided Eck with a window on the distinctive images through which Christians encounter Jesus. Although we have no precise parallel to the five faces of Shiva, Christians celebrate the Christ as a child, teacher, and healer, as the one who "suffered, died, and was buried," and as the one who was raised from the dead. Attending to Hindu forms of honoring Shiva and Krishna helped Eck to appreciate the specific images through which Christians learn the ways of discipleship.

For example, witnessing the way some Hindus venerate the child Krishna gave Eck a new appreciation for the Christ child. Many households contain images of Krishna crawling on his hands and knees with a ball of butter in one hand. In a commercial district of Banaras, Eck found a store exclusively devoted to clothing and adornments for the child Krishna. Charmed by the lightness and playfulness of such customs, Eck realizes that dressing up Krishna (like the devotion to the Infant of Prague among some Catholics) involves bringing one's affections and sensibilities to the service of God. A service in a rural village further stretches her imagination. After temple doors were opened to reveal Krishna, she sees two elderly priests bring out toys—silver tops and miniature cows—and play with them in front of

Krishna. "I was," she writes, "startled—dumb-founded really—at the notion that one might worship the Lord by offering the gift of play."[37]

In the playfulness of this moment at the temple, Eck discovered a new dimension of the incarnation: the use of familial, ritual language of love and hospitality toward God that enables people to "practice the presence" of the incarnate Lord of all life. Eck saw the attention lavished on the child Krishna complemented in the way the families loved their children. "A world in which children are the most vulnerable victims of poverty, malnutrition, and violence is surely in need of the refinement and enlargement of our capacity to see the Christ child."[38]

Similarly, the Hindu goddess Shakti, divine energy—"surging, mothering energy"—enlarged Eck's understanding of the Holy Spirit. It's not a simple analogy, as if Shakti is to Hindus what the Holy Spirit is to Christians, but rather that the Hindu expressions of Shakti might "push us toward a wider and more challenging understanding of the energy and power of the Holy Spirit."[39] For instance, the magnetism and vitality evident in the shrines to Shakti awaken in Eck a longing for Christian churches and holy places to have a similar sense of power and presence. The ways in which Hindus link Shakti with nature, most notably with the River Ganges, reveals the impoverishment in Christianity when people do not incorporate the icons of nature into their theological language:

> Nature does indeed reveal both the glory and terror of the Divine....there is no part of nature that carries for Christians the cultural power and mythic energy of the Ganges, as much as I love the Madison, the Gallatin, and the Blackfoot rivers [of Montana]. Why not? Perhaps those of us in the Western prophetic traditions have been afraid we will worship nature and not God. After all, the prophets of Israel embarked on a bold religious venture— to see the mighty power of God *not* in the mysteries of nature, as did their neighbors in the ancient world, but in the mystery of historical events....But "nature" and "history" are not true opposites....Both nature and history are revelatory. Both are infused with the energy and breath of God. If I can attest to the life of the Spirit in the daring history of the modern Christian ecumenical movement, I can also insist upon the presence of the Spirit in the cyclical renewal of nature....One cannot dismiss as pantheism the revelation of God in nature, the glimpse of nature streaming with the life of the Holy Spirit.[40]

Shakti, manifest in the image of the four-armed Kali, opens still another dimension of the Spirit to Eck. Kali is a terrifying figure in many ways, holding a cleaver in one hand and a severed head in another, yet also holding a lotus flower and gesturing in an inviting way. Her neck is circled with a garland of skulls and yet covered with red hibiscus. Kali reveals the "truth of divine power claiming the terrain of both life and death....[indicating] that the fullness of life includes both the flowering and the finality." Even the "spiritually benumbed" might recognize God's presence in a sunrise or in a cathedral, writes Eck.

> It is harder to sit still and be in God's presence in the places where we confront death. Most of us in the modern West run away from such places. We do not linger at the deathbed, in the morgue, at the graveside or the crematorium to wonder if the Holy Spirit might be there as well. But if faith is to sustain us at all, we will finally have to be open to the hovering Spirit in those very places that frighten us and make us tremble, to face the horror and trust the presence of God.[41]

Involvement in Hindu life did not simply enlarge Diana Eck's theological horizons; it animated her spirituality, giving it new depth and breadth. In particular, the mindfulness fostered by Hindu and Buddhist practices of meditation invites practitioners of all traditions of faith to a transformation of self. Spirituality—the cultivation of an awareness of God's presence, a disciplined nurturing of inner spiritual life that also has an outward dimension—transcends the boundaries of religions. Labels such as "Christian" or "Hindu" or "Buddhist" lose their relevance because practices such as sitting and breathing in order to center one's mind and heart belong to no one tradition. Christians who practice *vipassana* (mindfulness meditation) or *zazan* (sitting) might find themselves able to be still, "to be truly present to the Spirit, to cease clinging to concepts and images of Jesus, and to realize the living presence of God within."[42]

Of course, one can take on the practices of another tradition in a superficial manner, wrenching them from context and thereby both dishonoring the tradition in which they are integral and trivializing their transformative power. As Eck wisely reminds her readers, "crossing over into the spiritual life of another tradition is not a journey on which one embarks for quick answers or spiritual souvenirs." Belonging to two spiritual traditions risks either schizophrenia or dishonesty.[43] As her neighbor in Banaras, Bettina Bäumer, an Austrian Catholic who had entered deeply into Hindu spirituality, observes: "It is precisely here that I am completely naked and exposed and depend on nothing but divine grace." Yet Bäumer wonders if Christians aren't too much concerned with labels. "A spiritual dialogue," she says, "should precisely be beyond labels, enabling us to discover that perhaps the unknown pilgrim on the dusty and hot Indian road, in whose presence we feel 'our hearts burning,' is in reality He, the Risen One."[44]

A CATHOLIC-JEWISH ENCOUNTER I

The Sisters of Our Lady of Sion were founded in France in the 1840s for the express purpose of converting Jews to Catholicism. Now an international community of about nine hundred members, this congregation of religious women has undergone its own conversion, resulting in a radically changed view of mission. The Sisters of Sion at this time see themselves being called to promote understanding and justice for the Jewish community.[45] The dramatic tale of their transformation reveals both the church's teaching of contempt of Jews and its dawning realization that such teaching has had tragic consequences for the Jewish community as well as cast a long shadow on Christianity. Their metamorphosis, moreover, reveals the ways in which the dimensions of ambiguity and adaptability give depth to religious commitment.

Sion's founders, Theodore Ratisbonne (1802–1884) and his brother Alphonse (1814–1884), were upper-class, assimilated Jews from Strasbourg. Seeking to assuage their spiritual hunger, both were baptized and eventually became priests. With their conversion to Catholicism they adopted the prevalent theological view of supersessionism: Christ had made Judaism obsolete; the church had superseded Judaism.[46] In Theodore's words, "the ancient faith of the Jewish people was dead and the only possible means of reawakening it is in Christianity."[47] Thus, in 1843 Theodore began a catechumenate for Jewish children.

Four women who were deeply involved in this work of initiating young Jews into Christianity—Sophie Stouhlen, Louise Weywada, Anastasia Viala, and Flore Doutrelepont—formed a community among themselves and asked to be established as a religious order. Their consecration in 1846 included the promise "to work as zealously as possible for the conversion of the Jewish people, to vow my time, my care, my suffering, my prayers, my whole life to procuring their salvation by knowledge of the Gospel.[48] The Constitutions of 1874 specified their distinctive work: "Its particular aim is the sanctification of the Children of Israel. It is especially for this work of charity that the religious of Sion offer their prayers, works and sacrifices, consecrating themselves with unswerving fidelity to Jesus and Mary" (no. 5).

In actual fact, however, relatively few Sisters of Sion actively worked for the conversion of Jews.

The decision early in their history to open boarding schools meant that most members threw their energies into the demanding work of running schools. Their prayer, however, attested to the founding vision; the Rule specified various practices that embodied the commitment to conversion of Jews. It directed the sisters to recite "special invocations for the salvation of Israel every day." It mandated an addition to daily mass. In the solemnity of the moment after the consecration, the sisters were to chant a dirge three times, *"Pater, dimitte illis, non enim sciunt quid faciunt"* ("Father, forgive them for they do not know what they are doing" [Lk 23:34]). The Rule also instructed the sisters to make the Way of the Cross each Friday and to make this Act of Reparation at the end:

...The children of Israel did not know you. They denied the Holy and Just One. They immolated the author of life. They blasphemed your name without which there is no salvation....[T]hey distanced themselves from you who are the source of life, and they wander like straying sheep for more than two thousand years, in the shadow of death, without fatherland, without priests or prophets or altar or sacrifices. How long O Lord, will this just punishment last? Rise up, O God of Goodness, remember your mercy of old....look with kindness on the children

35

of Israel and convert them according to the promise made to Abraham and his posterity. Have pity on them because of Mary; hear the prayers of the daughters of Sion who repeat with humble confidence the last prayer of the crucified Jesus, *"Pater, dimitte illis, non enim sciunt quod faciunt."*

Such prayers shock our modern sensibilities. It is crucial to remember, however, that Sion merely took up in a focused way the church's enduring hostility toward Judaism, including its conviction that Jews must be converted. Let us recall that Catholics prayed for the "perfidious Jews" on Good Friday until Pope John XXIII removed the prayer from the liturgy in 1959:[49]

Let us pray also for the unfaithful Jews, that our God and Lord may remove the veil from their hearts; that they also may acknowledge our Lord Jesus Christ....Almighty and everlasting God, Who drivest not even the faithless Jews away from Thy mercy, hear our prayers, which we offer for the blindness of that people, that, acknowledging the light of Thy truth, which is Christ, they may be rescued from their darkness.

Sion was among the first groups in the church to recognize the grievous error of the theology such prayers represent. Three factors seem to have played an important role as they faced the way their congregation had lived out the church's teaching of *adversus Judaeos*. The most significant is that the Sisters of Sion in Europe had witnessed the devastating effect of the *Shoah* (Holocaust). A number had hidden Jews from the Nazis, and many more were deeply disturbed by what they had witnessed. The theological ferment in Catholicism, which would become more widespread through the Second Vatican Council (1962–1965), provided a second. Another contributing factor was Sion's presence in Israel. They had opened a house just west of Jerusalem in Ein Karem, and now they knew Jews as neighbors, not as an abstraction.

A rethinking of their mission first became evident in the late 1950s. In 1962, Sion's leadership, the general council, issued a letter to the congregation, asking that work and prayer for the conversion of Jews end and that instead the sisters work to counter antisemitism. They also recommended serious study of Judaism. We should note that the general council's letter preceded the watershed document of Vatican II, *Nostra Aetate,* by three years.[50]

This letter sent shock waves across the congregation. It was a bombshell for many, who saw deeply held beliefs challenged. One person told me, "My whole world caved in." Others welcomed the new direction. Whatever the initial reaction, ferment followed. My favorite anecdote comes from an Irish sister who was teaching in England during this period:

> I was teaching sixteen-year-olds, and one Monday morning one of the Anglicans announced she had been to Mass on Sunday. My ears pricked—a potential convert. However, on questioning her, I discovered she was talking of her Anglican Church, and at that time it even irked me to hear her call her service Mass! However, I began questioning her on the goings on in her Church, and kept getting the answers, "It's just like yours, only it's in English." My final query was to know if they offered Mass for special intentions. "Yes, they did." "Well, what was yesterday's intention?" "The conversion of Ireland."

That conversation gave her a new lens to look at her own vocation as a Sister of Sion. In experiencing another's zeal to convert the Irish, she began to question her own right to desire the conversion of others.

Sion's leadership sought to provide depth and breadth to such encounters by affirming the importance of pluralism and establishing Jewish-Christian work as a priority of the congregation. A general chapter of 1969–1970 recommended that 10 percent of the sisters under fifty be educated in order to specialize in Jewish-Christian relations. Centers were opened in Jerusalem and Rome, and teams of sisters were formed to work in "Jewish-Christian encounter" in cities such as London, Paris, Buenos Aires, and New York. Many sisters had their first opportunity to spend a significant amount of time in Israel; prior to pronouncing their final vows, all members now live in Israel for a period.

Sion's current Constitutions (1984) express a self-understanding radically different from the 1874 version. They speak of their apostolic life as characterized by a threefold commitment to the church, to the Jewish people, and to a world of justice, peace, and love. They articulate the commitment to Jews in the following fashion: "Our vocation gives us a particular responsibility to promote understanding and justice for the Jewish community, and to keep alive in the Church the consciousness that in some mysterious way, Christianity is linked to Judaism from its origin to its final destiny."

Sion's journey has not been easy. The general council's letter in 1962 and the changes unleashed by Vatican II caused considerable disequilibrium. Among other sources of consternation, the sisters had to learn to pray in a new way—the prayers cited above began to be removed in the late 1950s, and new forms had to develop. Yet their study of Judaism and involvement with Jews have given them a profound appreciation for Jewish spirituality even as it has raised many questions. Many of Sion's members express serious questions, for instance, about how to theologize in view of the *Shoah* and how Christians can reconcile the traditional teaching of the necessity of salvation in Christ with more inclusive views of salvation. Sion's delicate task is finding ways of honoring the wisdom and knowledge they find in Judaism with that of Catholicism and, more broadly, of Christianity. Their renewal, as one member has said, called them "from a conversionist stance, with clear boundaries and certitudes, to a dialogical way of life where the boundaries are far less distinct." This "dialogical way of life," she continues, "requires us to live side by side with a people different from ourselves, a community which describes the experience of God's own self in ways similar and related, yet distinct and quite different, a people which is yet intimately related to our identity as Church."

I believe the church has a great deal to learn from Sion about the practices of a dialogical way of life that will enable us to flourish in a religiously pluralistic world.

A Catholic-Jewish Encounter II

I draw the final example of a serious and sustained encounter between two religious traditions from my own experience in the Catholic-Jewish Colloquium. This project, which Sara S. Lee of Hebrew Union College, Los Angeles, and I conceived and directed from 1992 to 1995, involved twenty-two professional Catholic and Jewish educators from the northeastern quadrant of the United States. Funded by the Lilly Endowment Inc., we met for six intensive two-day sessions over a period of nearly two years, with our final session in November 1995. Although the grant has expired, the participants remain in touch with one another, and we hope to continue our study on a journey to Israel in January 1998.

Because Sara and I have written at length about this project and served as guest editors for an issue of the journal *Religious Education* around questions the colloquium raised, I will simply accentuate here the importance of educational process in the interreligious encounter.[51]

Our intentions appear even more ambitious in retrospect than we realized in the original design. We hoped not only to change the way the eleven religious educators from our own tradition understood the other's, but also to support them in pursuing the implications for their own religious self-understanding as well as for their work as educators. From the outset we recognized that the transformations we hoped to engender involved more than the acquisition of new concepts, as important as those were to our project.

We considered it of utmost importance to develop a rich environment in which participants might experience the stimulation and support of study with others, hone tools for deeper inquiry into another way of faith, and feel safe enough to risk laying aside misperceptions and shallowness.

We were mindful that the transformations we hoped participants would undergo were not symmetrical, with Christians needing to reconstitute their theology and Jews their self-understanding based on history. If Catholics were to rethink theological foundations often grounded in an inadequate understanding of Judaism, they required a sustained encounter with Judaism and Jews—with both the tradition itself and those who embody it. Firsthand experience by Catholics with contemporary Jews was essential to challenging residual ideas grounded in supersessionism and to gaining an understanding of Judaism as a complete and vibrant faith in its own right.[52]

Similarly, if Jews were to move beyond a singular perception of Christianity as a source of anti-Jewish belief and behavior to a fuller comprehension of Christianity in its historical and theological contexts, it was essential that they learn about Christianity on its own terms. Because Christianity's teaching of contempt has loomed so large in the Jewish experience, Jews needed a forum to discover Christianity from the inside in order to rework a self-identity often premised on being victims.

In sum, our desire was that Jews might experience the dynamics of Christian life as lived by knowledgeable, committed Catholics and that Catholics in turn might learn the vitality of Judaism as lived by knowledgeable, committed Jews so that both could engage in the kind of in-depth conversation that lies at the heart of genuine dialogue. This would happen, we believed, among people *studying in the presence of the other.* We wanted to transcend learning *about* the other, as important as that may be; rather, our interest lay in providing ways participants might deepen their knowledge of Judaism or Catholicism as *it was lived by informed, committed Jewish and Catholic educators.* In designing the colloquium to facilitate encounter with *the tradition as embodied in the other,* we developed a mode of dialogue we termed *interreligious learning,* which emphasizes the centrality of knowledge and study in structuring conversation across religious boundaries.

Two key elements of interreligious learning deserve explicit mention: the importance of study in the presence of the other and emphasis on the formative dimension of education. By emphasizing study, we respected the depth of knowledge the Christian-Jewish encounter demands and the complex character of the work of religious educators. The Lilly grant had enabled us to provide participants with a range of resources, including guest scholars and nineteen books on various dimensions of Jewish-Christian relations for their own collections. People prepared assiduously for each session, and we devoted substantial amounts of time to discussion. The mutual study of texts enabled participants to construct a common body of knowledge at the same time they were hearing diverse interpretations. Similarly, the attention we paid to the *formative dimension of the educational* process, including community-building and occasion for sharing one's personal immersion in the spirituality of the tradition, contributed significantly to the strong bonds participants developed among themselves.

We have ample testimony from the participants that the colloquium changed their understanding of the relationship between Judaism and Christianity. Catholics who brought to the colloquium a sense that Judaism was frozen in legalism or who regarded Judaism primarily as a preparation for or mere root of Christianity discovered it to be a living and vital tradition for which they felt great kinship. Participant Julie Collins, for example, tells of a small group sharing stories and symbols of sacred seasons. She had chosen to begin by reading the story of the Annunciation (Lk 1:26–38):

> In my mind's eye I pictured Mary sitting there, shy and overwhelmed, awash in the

radiance of the Angel Gabriel. All of a sudden, as I was narrating the tale of this young Jewish girl and her monumental "yes" to God, my throat closed, my eyes filled with tears and the letters blurred. I could barely continue. Stunned, I looked up into the faces of the two Jewish women in our group. It was as though Mary were in the room.[53]

As the colloquium opened them to a more textured portrait of Judaism and of its relation to Christianity, the Catholics realized the urgency of acquiring more adequate theological concepts, acknowledging more candidly the way in which anti-Judaism has shadowed Christian history, and finding ways to integrate their learning into their work as educators.

Jews whose perspectives on Christianity had been shaped primarily by knowledge of its hostility toward and persecution of Jews over the ages developed respect for its spiritual richness. One participant spoke of being jealous of the Catholic participants' ability to speak so readily of their spiritual experiences, another of feeling "exhilarated" yet "terrified" by the "meaningful, powerful and moving" ways in which Catholics spoke about Jesus.[54]

David Ellenson, a professor of Judaic thought, comments on the significance of this respect for and appreciation of Christianity:

...the Colloquium compelled the Jews to see their Catholic colleagues and friends in all their particularity as "Christian men and women." The Jewish participant in the Colloquium was forced to recognize that individuals may be good, decent, and spiritual not in spite of, but precisely because they are committed Christians. Christianity, these Jewish participants came to understand, consists of more than hatred for Jews. It comprises a force for good in the world. Constructing one's identity over against such persons is a much more complex and difficult task than establishing it over against a heinous caricature. It is no wonder, given the role that the Christian has traditionally played as the "preeminent other" for Jews in the construction of their own identity, that the effects of the Colloquium were "dizzying" upon the transformed sense of Jewish self-identity.[55]

A number of the Jewish participants told us that the anger, sadness, and shame they observed among the Catholics during the study of history had a freeing effect on them. Robert Tornberg writes, "Experiencing this allowed me to let go of much of my historical resentment and diminished the focus of my own victimization. This led to an unburdening of much of the anger I had carried around for years. Until I could release myself

46

from being a victim, I had no room to appreciate Christianity."[56]

Another outcome of the colloquium pertinent to my argument is the deep regard participants developed for the health and vitality of the other's community of faith. One Catholic spoke in his journal entry for Passover that he was remembering the name and face of each Jewish participant as he or she gathered with family and friends to commemorate that night different from all others. Another wrote of the profound effect of the colloquium as she viewed *Schindler's List* because she had "put names on those faces on the screen," and their names were those of the Jewish participants. "How could we have allowed this to happen to people who were just like my colleagues with whom I've studied, discussed, laughed, cried, for the past year? What can I do to make sure this never happens again?"[57] Jews spoke about the ways in which the bonds of community fostered a trust enabling them to take risks in the presence of the "other" not possible within their own community.[58] Another wrote that being with Catholics in the six sessions of the colloquium revealed "a richness in my Jewish soul I never anticipated. By honoring the distinctiveness of our respective communities, we made holy our differences even as we sanctified the bonds that link us as brother and sister in praise of the One God."[59]

47

The encounter with the other in the colloquium, as David Ellenson observed, led the participants into the "ineffability of God and of the mystery and infinity that lie at the heart of religion and culture, history and memory."[60] The colloquium was a profoundly religious experience; it drew its participants into the boundlessness of the Divine. It challenged participants to move beyond the narrow limits in which they confine the Holy One, to acknowledge in their heart of hearts that God, "the Mother and Father of us all, has many children. With each of them, and each branch of the larger family, God has a specific and precious relationship."[61]

To be sure, this experience was, to borrow Cynthia Reich's phrase, both exhilarating and terrifying. As Sandra Lubarsky has sagely noted, transformative dialogue can be simultaneously destabilizing and strengthening. Returning the ultimate to centrality can throw one off center. When dialogue renders a person more open and sensitive, then he or she becomes stronger. Paradoxically, however, the person becomes more fragile: "If the goal of religious traditions is not impenetrability or indestructibility, but receptivity to truth and beauty, then it is the tender strength of the butterfly, not the stone, that is to be valued."[62]

It was indeed the tender strength of the butterfly that the colloquium participants manifested.

After the first session, one participant said that it had come to her like a bolt from the blue that the colloquium "promises (threatens) to be life-changing. As I look at the roots of what I have believed and professed for all my life, there are some very problematic areas which emerge....This is...frightening, threatening...at the same time exciting, challenging and perhaps a new beginning."[63] Participants asked probing questions of themselves. One writes about questioning her entire identity as a follower of Christ; she began to wonder about her true faith: what did she really believe about Christ? About his birth, ministry, death and resurrection, salvific action?

> After much consternation and deep thought, I concluded with joy and great conviction that not only had I experienced God in the world but that more specifically I had *experienced Christ* in my own brokenness and in the brokenness of our world and in love that abounds when new life is shared. *The point here is that had I not been in the presence of others of deep faith who were questioning me to explain myself, I would not have needed to clarify my own beliefs for them nor for myself–nor would I have come to the depths of conviction that our study engendered.*[64]

Such a testimony might be regarded, suggests Sandra Lubarsky, as the kind of recommitment that invigorates our traditions of faith. But, continues Lubarsky, such recommitment leads to what Martin Buber calls "holy insecurity" because the price we pay for responsiveness and creativity is a lack of security:

> Religion is not only a cradle in which we calm our fears but a way of participating in the creativity that surrounds and infuses us and, yes, confuses us. Though we deeply desire security—of knowledge, of continued life, of love—it cannot be ours except paradoxically as we embrace creativity and its source. Dialogue with people of different faiths heightens the ambiguity in our lives because it is part and parcel of the creative action that defines life itself.[65]

THE FIVE ENCOUNTERS: KEY THEMES

In June 1996 Sara Lee and I worked at a further articulation of the concept of interreligious learning that had proven so important to the Catholic-Jewish Colloquium. The four characteristics we identified provide a useful heuristic for synthesizing key themes in the five stories I have told. Briefly, the four characteristics are: (1) the ability to enter another religious tradition without losing one's own boundaries, (2) the experience of investing in the health and welfare of another's religious tradition, (3) movement beyond tolerance to a genuine pluralism, and (4) keener awareness of both commonalities and differences between religious traditions.

First, we premised, interreligious learning enables persons to get inside of another's religious tradition without losing appropriate boundaries. This suggests a certain rhythm, what theologian John Dunne has called "passing over" and "coming home."[66] There is, on the one hand, involvement in another community's life, yet always a certain reticence, a recognition that one is an outsider and, hence, must return home. We see this in George Dardess' restraint about joining the Muslim prayer line *(salat),* and in a Jewish participant's "exhilaration and terror" when the Catholics spoke movingly to her about Jesus in the colloquium. Similarly, we recognize it in Diana Eck's knowledge that she shared the Hindus' sense of delight and revelation in the opening of the doors in the temple in the city of Trivandrum yet as a Christian experienced it differently from the Hindu worshipers pressed around her. We see it also in the deep appreciation for Jewish spirituality among the Sisters of Sion coupled with their sensibility that as Christians they ought not appropriate it—the traditions belong first and foremost to Jews. We likewise find it among some of the Jewish delegates in Dharamsala, who are both fascinated by

Buddhist mysticism yet unsure about the appropriateness of mystical practices in their own tradition.

All of these involve an element of strangeness, the recognition that the other tradition is powerful and inviting, yet simultaneously startling and alien. Theologian Darrell Fasching argues that Christians must replace the apologetic theology of an earlier era with an "alienated theology, a theology done as if we were aliens and strangers to our own stories and traditions, seeing them instead through the eyes of the stranger, who will be affected by them."[67] While I think Fasching's choice of the term *alienated theology* limits its usefulness, his argument nonetheless deserves our attention because it calls our attention to the importance of having other perspectives focused on our own. Similarly, educational philosopher Dwayne Huebner suggests that encounter with the stranger is fundamental to all educational processes in his description of education as the "meeting of the historically determined self with the new, the strange, the stranger" in such a way that the profound longing and thirst central to human life are "recognized as the source and goal of life."[68] Encounters with the stranger are all the more important in the religious realm because they are "pathways to new understandings of how God and human beings are in relationship."[69]

Second, interreligious learning invites people

to invest in the health and welfare of another's religious tradition. While this is most evident in the radically changed sense of mission among the Sisters of Sion—from converting Jews to Christianity to promoting justice for Jews in the church and world—it is apparent also in the other encounters. Although George Dardess does not report what effect his altered understanding of Islam had on his attitude toward the Islamic world, it seems reasonable to conclude that the friendships he developed through his study of the Qur'an have given him a profound respect for Islam. Profound respect, I suggest, is requisite for investing in the health and welfare of another. Such respect may also develop from awareness of the effect of suffering and exile, as in the dialogue between the Dalai Lama and the Jewish delegation. Or it may develop from the extended time spent learning from another culture, as in the many journeys Diana Eck has made to India as a scholar and seeker, not as a tourist. Or from the late-night exchanges of colloquium participants as they discovered the depth of one another's commitment to their respective communities of faith.

The investment in another tradition's well-being requires a belief in pluralism. As Rabbi Irving Greenberg says, "The big question on the religious agenda is how are people rooted in their own religion able to respond to others. We must learn to affirm our truth while doing justice to the other....God's will is for us to learn how to affirm our full truth doing full justice to the other, not partial justice or twisted justice or a secondhand treatment."[70] Once we come to believe, as does Greenberg, that "pluralism is God's will," then we will be able to care for the quality of religious commitment in other communities besides our own. In a global village, do we not all have a vested interest in the development of healthy religious communities rather than the pathological varieties that are responsible for so much division, hatred, and violence?

Third, interreligious learning transcends mere tolerance because it is oriented toward a genuine pluralism developed through serious study fused with a *hermeneutic of the affections.* It is grounded, moreover, in virtues such as *spiritual regret* and *holy envy.* Pluralism, as Diana Eck has clarified, is not merely a synonym for diversity but, rather, reflects active and positive engagement with religious claims and the fact of religious diversity. Nor is pluralism synonymous with tolerance: tolerance, though necessary in society, is too minimal an expectation because it "does not require us to know anything new, it does not even entertain the fact that we ourselves might change in the process."[71] Unlike tolerance, in which one resolves simply to live with difference, pluralism requires the pursuit of understanding. In distinction from relativism and syncretism, pluralism is built upon an encounter of commitments and a respect for difference that comes from extensive knowledge of one's tradition.[72]

Pluralism, in other words, does not magically happen because we recognize diversity; pluralism requires work and virtue. The work involves study in the fullest sense of that term—not only poring over unfamiliar texts or struggling to grasp an alien concept but also learning to hear with the ears of one's heart and to appreciate what the "other" holds dear. Thomas Green speaks of this as a "hermeneutic of the affections," a readiness to listen to the "loves of others."[73] Though I did not know the term at the time, I believe that the fundamental dynamic of the Catholic-Jewish Colloquium—study in the presence of the other—is absolutely critical in fostering a hermeneutic of the affections. The Eck and Kamenetz books testify eloquently to their experiences of learning the loves of Hindus and Buddhists. Moreover, I might add, the readiness to listen to the loves of others also requires attending to what causes them to suffer. I think of the remark of a Sister of Sion: "Jewish experience, marked as it is by suffering, 'rubs off' on us in ways that go beyond our conscious awareness."

Undergirding the hermeneutic of the affections are two virtues important for fostering a religious pluralism: spiritual regret and holy envy. Religion scholar Lee Yearley defines *spiritual regret* as "one of those virtues that concerns the appropriate response to the recognition that extremely varied, legitimate religious ideals exist and that no person can possibly manifest all of them."[74] I can think of no better illustration than the comment of a rabbi in the colloquium: "When I study Torah, I recite a blessing over the study of God's word. As we studied the Christian scriptures, I felt a need to say a blessing as well. The traditional blessing would not have been appropriate. But I felt sad I had no blessing to say."[75]

Yearley's own example of spiritual regret is similar. He had spent two early-morning hours in Korea on a high cliff looking at the Sokkurum Buddha, a large granite statue carved in the eighth century, a figure that drew his attention with "a magnetic power" and that generated a "mysterious kind of peace." Says Yearley: "The spiritual vision presented there was as powerful and as tempting as I have ever seen. Yet I wanted it neither for myself nor for those about whom I care most. I wanted the religious goods expressed in the Sokkurum Buddha to exist, and even to be incarnated by many people, and yet did not want the people I cared most about to possess them."[76] The value of spiritual regret, Yearley claims, is that it corrects our unwillingness to face fully the implications of pluralism; it likewise corrects the propensity to forms of idolatry or envy in which we see diverse spiritual goods only in our own image or feel resentment toward spiritual goods we do not possess.

New Testament scholar Krister Stendahl offers a complementary term, "holy envy." Having heard his term only in oral presentation and not having found a written definition, I understand Stendahl to mean the experience of something so profound in the beliefs, rituals, polity, or practices of another tradition that one wishes her or his own community of faith also had (or practiced) it—and yet refrains out of respect for the other. Diana Eck describes her former colleague's term as "the appreciative love one has toward the mysteries of another faith."[77] One of the colloquium participants provides an illustration of holy envy:

I was also becoming quite conscious of my "jealousy" of the Catholic participants' ability to speak so easily about their spiritual experiences. I was, therefore, quite surprised when my roommate expressed his own jealousy over the depth of learning the Jewish participants had about their texts and the intellectual side of religion. When I reacted to this and shared my own sense of what I was lacking, we both felt validated in who we are. We also learned something important about the strength of the other and understood that we could help each other learn to "fill in the gaps" we each sensed we were missing.[78]

The concepts of spiritual regret and holy envy express an important dimension of interreligious learning: when we drink deeply from the wells of another tradition, we may see more clearly distortions and deficiencies in our own. Painful though such a vision may be, it does discourage the inclination to make idols of our own religious beliefs and practices. It also may galvanize us to integrate appropriately into our own tradition some dimension of what we have admired of the other. Thus, for example, Catholics edified by the deep knowledge of Judaica manifested by the Jewish participants in the colloquium expressed the desire to commit themselves to more serious study.

Fourth, interreligious learning sharpens awareness and significance of both differences and commonalities. As Kamenetz reports, in discovering some of the differences between Judaism and Tibetan Buddhism—such as the latter's stress on the separation between culture and religion, religion and nationalism, religion and daily life—he also discovered Judaism anew. In the light of Tibetan Buddhism, Kamenetz realized that the religion of his birth was not simply an ethnicity or an identity, but "a way of life and a spiritual path, as profound as any other."[79] The Dalai Lama provided him and others in the delegation "a pool of nectar to look into, sweeter than a mirror, so that we Jews could see ourselves, not necessarily as we are, but as we might be."[80]

George Dardess testified that his study of the Qur'an made him "more joyfully and wonderingly a Christian than before" because it enlarged his sense of the Word of God. Yet for him God's Word in the Qur'an was not transformative in the same way or to the same degree as in Christianity. Diana Eck is mindful that for all the analogies between Hindu Gods and images by which Christians think of Jesus there are still profound differences. To probe those differences is to deepen understanding of one's own tradition of faith.

Accompanying the more acute awareness of difference and commonality is a keener awareness that what one says about the other should be able to be said in the presence of the other. I know, for example, that the Catholic participants in the colloquium will never again teach that "Jews think" or "Judaism is" without remembering the Jews they came to know; they realize now that whatever claims they make about Jews and Judaism must be able to be said in their presence.

Finally, it seems appropriate to return to Kamenetz's intriguing notion that the Dalai Lama had revealed Judaism to them not simply as it is but *as it might be*. Perhaps we might claim that interreligious learning at its best reveals the potential in our own traditions by evoking what is deepest and most powerful in our religious commitments. It calls forth what is best in our faith.

4. A CATHOLIC'S ENCOUNTER WITH JUDAISM

I grew up in the Pacific Northwest, which, while religiously diverse, also has the highest proportion of persons who are not affiliated with church or synagogue. As a consequence, I took for granted, both in my family and beyond it, a range of religious belief and practice, as well as lack of belief and observance. Although there weren't many Jews in my hometown of Seattle, it may be that my attraction to Judaism is related to the fact that the one Jew I did know owned a candy store and shared abundantly from it! Pauline Lee, a member of our extended family though not a blood relation, arrived at every family celebration with an enormous box of nuts and candies—pecan rolls and fudge for my father, chocolate creams for my grandmother, licorice for all the women (an addiction apparently passed down the maternal line) and an array of other candies for all to feast on. I remember how she would arrive exhausted for dinner on Christmas and Easter, with hands and feet swollen from packing boxes

61

and long hours behind the counter. I remember, too, the story told about my grandfather helping her to establish her business, including his advice to change her name from Solomon to Lee to avoid discrimination. It was, I believe, my first awareness of antisemitism. I don't think I quite understood how it was she was Jewish but not religious; only much later did I learn of her yearning to know more about Judaism. When I went to Israel for the first time in January 1979, Pauline asked me to buy her a *mezuzah*. It was a purchase that gave me great pleasure.

My high school years coincided with the Second Vatican Council (1962–1965), and its ecumenical and interreligious spirit excited me. A group of us at the Catholic school I attended, Holy Names Academy, organized a dialogue day with the youth group from the synagogue a mile or so away, Temple De Hirsch Sinai. Other than that event, which impressed upon me the fact that Jews and Catholics thought in quite different categories, I had no contact with knowledgeable, observant Jews. In college, however, I encountered the thought of Rabbi Abraham Joshua Heschel, initially through his classic work, *The Prophets*. When I began teaching high school in 1969, I continued to study some of his other writings; I was awestruck by his profundity.

When I arrived in New York City to begin graduate school in 1974, I soon realized I had moved to Heschel's neighborhood. In fact, the dining room of the Dominican convent where I lived had a splendid view of the quadrangle of the Jewish Theological Seminary, where he had taught, and I met people who had been his students or colleagues. How I envied them, because Rabbi Heschel had died in 1972. What I would have given just to see him on the street![81]

Fortunately, however, I came to know other Jews and at the same time learn more about Judaism through my studies. A classmate from Teachers College to whom I had grown close invited me to her family's seder in Dayton, Ohio, an experience I found deeply moving. My move to Boston in 1977 to teach at Boston College continued this opening to Jewish life, as I came to know many Jews, as well as Christians knowledgeable about Judaism, and to work with organizations committed to increasing understanding between Jews and Christians. I also had the opportunity to spend time in Israel, initially going with a group of Jews and Catholics from Boston, then spending a semester in the early 1980s; a colleague and I also took groups on several occasions. Before I knew it, I had become deeply involved in the realm of Jewish-Christian relations, an involvement that experience in the Catholic-Jewish Colloquium deepened and extended immeasurably.

These autobiographical fragments help to frame my remarks in this final section. I am not a scholar trained in comparative religion, as is Diana Eck, nor someone who has been tutored intensely in the recitation of another's sacred text, as has George Dardess. Rather, I am simply a Catholic for whom Jewish life has become revelatory. My encounter with Jews and Judaism has opened new depths of God's elusive presence and challenged me to rethink my understanding of Christianity. It has disclosed the sinful, shadow side of the church—a knowledge I carry with shame and sorrow. Paradoxically, my involvement with Jews has also heightened my appreciation for some of the distinctive contributions of Christian traditions. Often that appreciation has grown from questions Jews have asked about Christianity. I think of a statement from the Catholic bishops of France that Jews "pose questions to us Christians which touch on the heart of our faith."[82] I feel privileged to know people who ask me such profound questions.

As a theologian, I have learned the truth of Clark Williamson's argument that "Conversation with Jews is indispensable to understanding Christian faith;...the historical evidence massively attests to the fact that apart from listening to and talking with Jews, we will misunderstand the Christian faith and act on our misunderstandings."[83] Not only do I share Williamson's conviction that conversation with Jews is requisite for understanding Christianity, but I believe encounter with Judaism has tremendous power to nurture healthy religious commitment among Christians—a conviction borne out in my personal experience.

What, then, does it mean for Christians to "converse" with Jews?

As a case in point, let me first reflect on ways my encounter with Jews and Judaism affects my commitments as a practicing Catholic. Then I will return to the premise that Sara Lee and I posed about the Christian task vis-à-vis Judaism, namely, that Christians need to rework their theology insofar as it is grounded in a superficial or inadequate understanding of Judaism. After I describe some of the theological horizons that recent scholarship extends, I will conclude with a word about educating for religious commitment in light of the interreligious encounter.

LEARNING FROM JEWS: A CALL FOR CHRISTIANS

In retrospect, I recognize that my involvement in Jewish life happened rather than resulted from any systematic plan. First there was our family friend Pauline, then the impact of the ecumenical impulse of the Second Vatican Council, followed by encounter with the thought of Rabbi Heschel. Friendships with Jews developed during my studies in the mid-1970s, and the circle of friends and colleagues widened during my seventeen years at Boston College and during my trips to Israel. My current appointment at Union Theological Seminary expands that network, including my involvement with colleagues across the street at Jewish Theological Seminary, where I serve as an adjunct professor. Of great personal significance is the deep bond of trust and affection that more than a decade of work with Sara Lee has given me.

So I have been brought gradually and unscientifically into Judaism: invited to table for *Shabbat* and seder in homes of friends, walking atop the walls of Jerusalem's Old City, using my halting Hebrew in synagogue services, meeting monthly for six years with a Jewish-Catholic women's group, and absorbing Jewish culture—Yiddish terms and eastern European foods, dialectic, and humor. Throughout I've read in order to understand more fully what this involvement might mean, but my study has been as unscientific as my engagement. At times it's been theological and historical, as I've developed an intense interest in the interaction of our two communities of faith in the first four centuries. It has ventured more widely as well, as I've read about Jewish practices, historical and religious studies of Israel, Jewish communal life, education, and feminism. Such an unscientific formation leaves many important areas untouched, such as study of the Talmud. Quite clearly, I am not a scholar of Judaism;

rather, my study to date has been directed toward giving my involvement greater depth and breadth. What my engagement and study have done is discipline and animate my commitments as a Christian.

How so? My encounter with Judaism has forced me to look squarely at the way Christians over time have treated "the other." It has breathed new life into a central religious practice, Sabbath-keeping, and lifted up some important dimensions of prayer. My encounter with Judaism, above all, has challenged me to a deeper relationship with God. It also has, following Kamenetz (above, p. 59), revealed Catholicism *as it might be,* evoking at times what is deepest and most powerful in my home tradition. A word on each.

Christians typically think of Jews as the people of the Old Testament. Unless they know Jews personally or have some other entrée into the Jewish world, they tend not to think of Judaism as a vital way of life in the contemporary world. They generally know even less about the history of the interaction between our two communities. Jews often understand relatively little about Christianity, but nearly all know the basic contours of that history—a story with scandalously many tales of Christian insensitivity, ignorance, domination, violence, and persecution. Any Christian who engages with Jews must learn this history.

And so I have. It is the major reason, I believe,

for my argument that healthy religious commitments must be characterized by ambiguity—by a willingness to be challenged by complexity and to dwell in one's own tradition without fear. As historian Edward Flannery observes, "It is an observable fact that it is often the rigid Christian who is the most likely candidate for antisemitism."[84] The dimension of ambiguity is all the more important when a group achieves political dominance. Polemics and power are a dangerous combination, particularly when ignorance about Judaism harmonizes with a superficial grasp of Christianity. Facing our history with Jews and Judaism, particularly in the *Shoah,* is not a task that will allow us to feel good about ourselves—so seekers may be put off—but it is essential to our maturity. Unless we face our shadow side, our proclamation of the gospel will ring hollow; unless we confess that God's ways transcend our finite understandings, our commitment will be shallow. Until we acknowledge the consequences of triumphalist rhetoric combined with political power, Christian involvement in the public square will rightly be suspect.

One of the tragic consequences of the Christian teaching of contempt for Judaism is our blindness to its religious depth. We have only to look to splendid teachers like Rabbi Irving Greenberg to be drawn into the profundity of the Jewish holidays.[85] And, once drawn in, we may find ourselves examining our own religious practice, as I did when I read Heschel's monograph on the Sabbath. Consider the following passage:

They who want to enter the holiness of the day must first lay down the profanity of clattering commerce, of being yoked to toil. They must go away from the screech of dissonant days, from the nervousness and fury of acquisitiveness and the betrayal in embezzling their own life. They must say farewell to manual work and learn to understand that the world has already been created and will survive without the help of humankind. Six days a week we wrestle with the world, wringing profit from the earth; on the Sabbath we especially care for the seed of eternity planted in the soul. The world has our hands, but our soul belongs to Someone Else. Six days a week we seek to dominate the world, on the seventh day we try to dominate the self.[86]

Heschel's reflections struck a responsive chord: I knew what it felt like to be yoked to toil (even if not manual labor), to feel as if there were no respite from work. I began to think seriously about Sabbath. Over the years I studied commentaries on the "Ten Words" (or Commandments, Exodus 20:1–17 and Deuteronomy 5:6–12), read Jewish and Christian explorations of the Sabbath,

69

noted how Jews observed (or not) the Sabbath in various ways, learned from Christians who practice Sabbath-keeping (such as many Sisters of Sion), and gave serious thought to the rhythm of work and rest in my life. I realized how readily work had become an idol in my life. I listened to the admonition of Luke Timothy Johnson: "Observe the way we organize the time and space available to us. The pattern reveals what is ultimate for us, our functional god."[87] Dorothy Bass extends Johnson's counsel:

> To act as if the world cannot get along without our work for one day in seven is a startling display of pride that denies the sufficiency of our generous Maker. To refrain from working—not every day, but one in seven—opens the temporal space within which glad and grateful relationship with God and peaceful and appreciative relationship with nature and other people can grow. Refraining from work on a regular basis should also teach us not to expect too much work from others.[88]

And so I stopped working on Sundays. I try to participate in a Eucharistic liturgy that is life-giving rather than an obligatory "going to mass." I engage in activities that are renewing, such as meals or phone conversations with friends. I do things I find restful, like cooking, walking, reading—and yes, watching football or basketball! I try to ready my spirit for the week to come, such as attending choral vespers by candlelight at the nearby Episcopal cathedral, St. John the Divine—the equivalent for me of participating in the *havdalah* service that concludes *Shabbat* for Jews.

Jewish prayer also evokes deep resonance in me.[89] Although I do not share the intense desire to pray with Jews and to share in the life of the synagogue that a few of my Christian friends do, I nevertheless feel my prayer is enriched by what I know of Jewish prayer. For example, in one community where I lived, we took turns preparing morning prayer. When it was my turn, I occasionally used excerpts from a weekday prayer book of the Reform Jews. Our community, nearly all of whom were involved in academic life, loved to pray this together:

> A spark of the divine flame glows within us all. We give thanks for the gift of reason that enables us to search after knowledge. May our use of this gift make Your light burn ever more brightly within us.
> *Blessed is the Eternal Source of wisdom and knowledge.*
> May our pride of intellect never be an idol turning us away from You. And as we grow

in knowledge, may we remain aware of our own limitations.

Blessed is the God of forgiveness and understanding.

May the beauty and mystery of the world move us to reverence and humility. O let the tree of knowledge bear good fruit for us and our children.

Blessed is our God from whom all blessings flow.

And let the consciousness of Your Presence be the glory of our lives, making joyous our days and years, and leading us to a clearer understanding of Your will.

Blessed is our God who hearkens to prayer.[90]

Similarly, I often use Marge Piercy's poem "Nishmat"—evoking the prayer *Nishmat kol hai* ("the breath of every living thing") from the Sabbath service—for my own morning prayer. The fourth stanza alone evokes much reflection:

We are given the wind within us, the breath
to shape into words that steal time, that touch
like hands and pierce like bullets, that waken
truth and deceit, sorrow and pity and joy,
that waste precious air in complaints, in lies,
in floating traps for power on the dirty air.
Yet holy breath still stretches our lungs to sing.[91]

When I study scriptural texts, I draw upon the resources of Jewish scholars nearly as often as

Christian ones, and my library includes an increasing number of meditative works by Jewish thinkers such as Carol Ochs, Daniel Gordis, and David Wolpe.[92]

I have a certain reserve when it comes to using Jewish prayers and even imagery distinctive to Jewish life. Belonging as I do to a tradition that proclaimed itself the fulfillment of Judaism, I am aware that Jews may see my use of their prayers as another example of Christian appropriation of their tradition. I have participated in various rituals and liturgies in which people appropriated rituals from another's tradition—most recently from Native Americans—without regard for the context of that ritual, and I find myself increasingly uncomfortable. However well intentioned, I believe using another's rituals without a deep knowledge of their context and appropriate use manifests a lack of sensitivity. Those attracted to aspects of another's tradition need always to leaven their attraction with the virtues of spiritual regret and holy envy. Moreover, because I am not learned in Jewish liturgy, I am cautious in employing Jewish prayers beyond the privacy of my home, lest I do injustice to the context in which they are prayed. This, I believe, is a caution born of spiritual regret.

My attraction to Jewish prayer suggests that I have found Judaism a catalyst for a deeper relationship with God. In my experience, Jews are generally more reticent about God talk than are we Christians. It seems to me that at least some of this reserve follows from more explicit acknowledgment of God's presence in hiddenness. Christians, too, carry this awareness, but we tend to emphasize God's revelation in Jesus to such a degree that we are less attentive to the elusive character of the Divine Presence. I have found, for example, Everett Fox's translation of the enigmatic phrase of Exodus 3:14 (the Hebrew transliteration *ehyeh asher ehyeh* is typically rendered, "I am who am") as "I will be-there-howsoever I will be-there." Fox notes that he is following Martin Buber and Franz Rosenzweig on this; it might mean something like "my name is not a magical handle through which I can be conjured up; I am ever present."[93] His translation emphasizes the mystery of God, the One who is incomprehensible yet present in ways beyond our imagining.

God's presence as "I will be-there-howsoever I will be-there" has other dimensions that I find Judaism quite bold in addressing. A brief story speaks to my point. Last summer I spent a few days with two longtime friends enjoying theater at the Shakespeare Festival in Stratford, Ontario. During our long drives to and from Stratford, we shared aspects of our lives that our busy calendars and geographic distance from one another seldom permit us to speak about. On this particular evening, Kathleen, a historian and college president who has had cancer, asked the two of us how theologians today were thinking about Divine Providence. There was an uncharacteristic silence for quite some time. Finally, I found myself voicing the view that I had learned a great deal from Jews who refused to turn aside from the *Shoah,* who questioned God's absence from the camps, who had stared deeply into the abyss and could simultaneously interrogate God and affirm belief. I realized I had few answers to give Kathleen—only a testimony that faith in God does not preclude questioning, that belief in Divine Providence takes one into the realm of that holy insecurity of which Martin Buber spoke.[94] In retrospect, I realize how grateful I am to have encountered Jewish writers who refuse to turn aside from the difficult dimensions of faith.[95] I realize as well how appreciative I am of the Jewish tradition of arguing with God—a tradition I believe we Christians must also claim if our religious commitments are to be healthy.[96]

What I have learned from Jews is difficult to put into words; so, too, is the deepened appreciation for Christianity's distinctive traditions that my encounter with Judaism has fostered. Three aspects of Christianity come to mind in this regard: discipleship in the way of Jesus, the symbolism of the cross, and the language of the Spirit.

Christology is obviously one of the most controversial and debatable topics between Jews and

Christians. Let me acknowledge here that I, like most Christians involved in Jewish-Christian dialogue, have many questions about the meaning of the Christ that are not readily resolved. What does it mean for us today, for instance, to claim that Jesus is the Son of God through whom we are saved? What does it mean for us to proclaim that Jesus is the Messiah, the agent of God's justice and reconciliation, when the world remains so broken and divided? Questions like these may well pursue me throughout my life, but study and dialogue with Jews have also encouraged me to deepen my sense of what discipleship entails. The study I have done on Jesus in his first-century context has enlivened him for me, given me a clearer and more compelling vision of what his ministry might have meant.[97] At the same time, it has made my understandings more tentative. I often think of Daniel Harrington's observation: "A good deal more is known about Palestinian Judaism in Jesus' day than was known forty years ago. But in another sense we *know less.* Or at least we are less confident about simple and neat pictures."[98] Precisely because we cannot justify uncomplicated understandings of the Christ, we need to live with a degree of ambiguity.

It is not only with regard to Jesus that Judaism has made me less confident about "simple and neat pictures." It has also shaped the way I understand the central symbol of Christianity, the cross. In studying the history of the relationship of our two communities, I was appalled by the connection between the church's anti-Judaism and its use of the cross. There is, for example, the accusation, first attributed to Melito of Sardis in the late second century, that Jews had murdered God and were, therefore, a community condemned. There were the Crusaders who wore the cross emblazoned on their tunics even as they slaughtered Jews in Germany en route to liberate the Holy Land from the "infidels," the Muslims. There were the mystics of the High Middle Ages who developed an emotional cult of the passion at the very point when Christian persecution of Jews was at its height. There was the cross erected by the Carmelites at Auschwitz in 1989. These and other instances horrified me with their disfigurement of our sacred symbol—so much so that I was prepared to argue for replacing it with alternative symbols.

During this period I had an experience in which I realized that the cross was so inextricably linked to Christian life that it could not (and should not) be laid aside. One Sunday morning several years ago at the parish I then belonged to, I became caught up in the moving ritual marking the acceptance of candidates for baptism (catechumens). In the second part of the ritual, the presider traces the cross on the forehead of the candidates and prays for each. Then the candidates' teachers and sponsors sign the cross over their ears, eyes, lips, breast, shoulders, hands, and feet, respectively:

Receive the sign of the cross on your ears,
that you may hear the voice of the Lord.
Receive the sign of the cross on your eyes,
that you may see the glory of God.
Receive the sign of the cross on your lips,
that you may respond to the word of God.
Receive the sign of the cross over your heart,
that Christ may dwell there by faith.
Receive the sign of the cross on your shoulders,
that you may bear the gentle yoke of Christ.
Receive the sign of the cross on your hands,
that Christ may be known in the work which you
    do.
Receive the sign of the cross on your feet,
that you may walk in the way of Christ.[99]

I knew in that moment that the cross was a symbol too bound up with my faith to be laid aside.

Having to face the way Christians had betrayed the cross even as I came to a new appreciation of its power for Christians has been an important journey for me. Not only has it provided me with a heightened appreciation for the complexity of symbols, but it has also stimulated me to reflect more deeply on the meaning of the passion and death of Jesus. Questions asked of me by Jews have encouraged my reflection. I think of a question addressed to me after a talk in a synagogue two years ago, "What is it that Christians find so compelling in the passion accounts?" An obvious question, perhaps. So obvious I'd never given it much thought—but one that is much on my mind now. As the bishops of France said in 1973, Jews "pose questions to us Christians which touch on the heart of our faith."

Beyond the questions there is the silence, because at times the asymmetry of Judaism and Christianity means that we confront understandings and practices so distinctive in each tradition that even the most articulate explanation does not suffice. Recently, for example, I was involved in a discernment process that followed the broad contours of the spirituality of St. Ignatius of Loyola as practiced by the Society of Jesus (Jesuits) and adapted by women. It was a deeply moving, if difficult, experience. Discernment in this mode is a way of honoring each person's interior freedom in the process of seeking the common good. Yet I found myself unable to share much about the dynamics of this process with Jewish friends because so much of it is connected to distinctively Christian language about the movement of the Spirit. Such occasions, however, are less occasions for sadness at the inability to cross the boundaries of one's religious traditions and more moments of realization of what is best and most powerful in

Christian life. The practice of discernment of spirits reveals a way of wisdom distinctive to Christianity.

Roberta Bondi writes that the work of "real" theology is "learning to see God and understand reality and ourselves as we really are in order that we may grow and thrive and become the loving people God wants us to be."[100] This describes as well my encounter with Judaism. It has engendered at times considerable dissonance as I've faced my parochialisms about God, reality, and the Christian community.[101] It has, in Diana Eck's words, "enabled me to understand my own faith more clearly and has required that I understand my own faith differently" (above, p. 23). Involvement with Jews has simultaneously opened a whole new realm of questions about the multiform ways in which the world's peoples approach the Divine. In fact, I am now far more drawn to other religious traditions because of what my engagement with Judaism has meant. Though I know little about Hinduism, for instance, I "got" Eck's book because she spoke to my own encountering God in Judaism. Judaism has opened new vistas on God and God's diverse peoples. It has also challenged me to rethink my theological foundations as a Christian.

GROUNDING CHRISTIANITY IN A
FAITHFUL PORTRAIT OF JUDAISM:
THE THEOLOGICAL TASK

I was formed by what might be called the conventional account of Christian origins, a synthesis of the teaching that many, if not most, Christians learned in one form or another and that has a deep hold on the imagination.[102] Here's the kind of teaching that many of us inherited in one variant or another:

> God, creator of all life, called the Jewish people to be his people, making a covenant with them that they might be a "light to the nations." Yet they failed to keep this covenant faithfully, so God promised to send them a Messiah. Jesus, the long-awaited Messiah foretold by the prophets, preached a gospel of love and freedom that transcended the confines of the Law, especially as interpreted by the Pharisees. He was crucified at Jewish hands because they rejected his message and denied his divinity. Thus, God "spoke to our ancestors," as the writer of Hebrews puts it, "in many and various ways by the prophets, but in these last days he has spoken to us by a Son, whom he appointed heir of all things, through whom he also created the worlds" (1:1).

So Christianity, the religion of Jesus, not only originated in Judaism but fulfilled it. The divinity of Christ was the defining issue, the basis for the break with the synagogue. By A.D. 70 the two were definable religions, clearly differentiated from each other. Thus, they went their separate ways, with Christianity flourishing in the Roman Empire, while Judaism diminished in importance.

A number of corollaries about Judaism usually accompanied the conventional account, although these corollaries are today generally taught with less force and with less frequency. They often appear in subtler forms.

◆ The Jews did not take to heart the warnings of their prophets to obey the covenant; their covenant is therefore abrogated.
◆ The Jews did not correctly understand the prophecies about the Messiah. Expecting a royal, glorious Messiah, they could not recognize Jesus as Messiah.
◆ Postexilic Judaism in the sixth century B.C. was legalistic, with undue emphasis on laws of purity and with minute regulations about such primitive practices as animal sacrifice.
◆ The Pharisees, source of so much opposition to Jesus, represented the epitome of legalism.

Theologically, the conventional account is supersessionist, that is, it rests on the premise that God's revelation in Jesus Christ supersedes the revelation to Israel. From this premise follows the understanding of the relationship between Old and New Testaments: they are related as seed to flower, shadow to reality, as promise to fulfillment. Similarly grounded in supersessionism is the claim that the church has replaced the Jews as God's people because the Jews rejected God's revelation in Jesus Christ. The church is the New Israel. In short, supersessionism is the seedbed of anti-Judaism.

Developments in biblical studies in the past thirty years, however, have made supersessionism obsolete, and a host of theological studies testify to the serious and profound rethinking among many Christian scholars.[103] The literature reveals, for example, the diverse understandings of messianism in early Judaism, the New Testament's polemical presentation of the Pharisees, the complex interaction between certain Jewish leaders and the Roman rulers in the crucifixion of Jesus, and the prolonged and complicated parting of the ways between Christianity and Judaism.[104] It also exposes the bias many feminist Christian theologians have manifested toward Judaism.[105] Furthermore, ecclesial documents across a wide range of Christian traditions offer evidence of ways in which the churches are rethinking their relationship with Judaism.[106] Publishers, particularly in Catholic circles, have revised textbooks in order that they might conform with these developments.[107]

Yet in part because of its embodiment in hymns and other devotional customs, this conventional account has had tremendous staying power. We still sing of the need to "ransom captive Israel / that mourns in lonely exile here / until the Son of God appear," and "Isaiah 'twas foretold it." Homilists still include in their Advent preaching the claim that the Jews didn't recognize Jesus as the Messiah because they were looking for a royal, glorious Messiah, and they continue to take the New Testament's characterization of the Pharisees as hypocritical legalists at face value. During Holy Week, most Christians hear the proclamation of the passion accounts without any realization of what Christians of an earlier era did to Jews, the "Christ-killers," during this time.

The simplicity of the conventional account also explains its hold on the Christian imagination. It offers an orderly picture of the beginnings of Christianity, a clear rationale for the departure from the synagogue, and an unequivocal warrant for distinct identity. Anti-Judaism—a mode of oppositional identity for the early church—developed in a community needing to draw clear and impermeable boundaries for its own survival.[108] Moreover, the early church couched its anti-

Jewish pronouncements in the rhetorical conventions of the day, which required the vilification of one's opponents.[109] Consequently, anti-Judaism became a powerful force in shaping the identity of a minority group that did not become a licit religion until the Constantinian era.[110]

Without doubt, a clear and distinct boundary can be established by polemics undergirded by inadequate historical analysis and questionable interpretations. Today, however, clear and impermeable boundaries no longer suffice. We know the evil that religious polemics have engendered. We know more about the complex world out of which Christianity emerged and in which Christians are no longer a minor religious group seeking legitimacy. We know the imperative for religious leadership in a world in which too many persons and groups have as yet to learn to tolerate those of another faith, let alone develop the appropriate attitudes and skills for fostering pluralism.

EDUCATING FOR RELIGIOUS COMMITMENT IN A PLURALISTIC WORLD

As a religious educator, I believe one of the most pressing questions we must address is this: What sort of education and formation in faith enables persons to participate intelligently in a religiously pluralistic society? I have suggested earlier that serious and sustained encounter with another religious tradition is critical to fostering intelligent participation in religious pluralism. It forms commitments that are at once clear and ambiguous, rooted and adaptive, even as it animates a more vital understanding and practice of one's own tradition of faith. I have substantiated this claim by describing ways in which encounters with persons of other religious traditions have profoundly shaped how they understand and practice their own tradition. It is evident in each case that thoughtful encounter with another religious tradition has enabled these persons to understand their home tradition more clearly even as it has required them to understand it differently.

The leadership in our churches is rightly concerned about the sorry state of religious literacy among its members, particularly the younger ones. But our efforts to convey Christian life in clear and compelling ways must be grounded in truth—and that means attentiveness to a God beyond all imagining and thus to a God beyond the bounds of the Christian imagination. Those of us who believe, with Rabbi Greenberg, that "pluralism is God's will" (above, p. 54) must incarnate that claim in the way we live and teach our faith. Educational practice in the church rests on our understanding of God and of God's relationship with the many peoples of this world.

One clue for how we might educate lies in an exhortation from the Vatican's Commission on Religious Relations with the Jews: "Religious teaching, catechesis and preaching should be a preparation not only for objectivity, justice and tolerance but also for understanding and dialogue. Our two traditions are so related that they cannot ignore each other. Mutual knowledge must be encouraged at every level."[111] Were we to consider "understanding and dialogue" a mandate for those with educational responsibilities in the churches, then it would obligate us to at least two commitments: engagement with the "other" and employment of pedagogical practices that enable persons to engage in "border crossing." A brief word on each.

Might we not assert that in a pluralistic world, no Christian can responsibly educate other Christians if he or she has not encountered in some significant way the beliefs and practices of a religious "other." It is, after all, the "other" or the "stranger" who may reveal to us aspects of the Divine Presence we never dreamed of, or who may illumine our way of faith by asking questions that shatter our complacency and challenge us to look more profoundly into our own tradition. Moreover, "After Auschwitz, nothing in the Gospels can be considered the word of God that does not teach hospitality to the stranger, beginning with the Jews."[112]

More than engagement with the "other," however, is requisite for education in the churches. We must model our engagement in our teaching. That is, we must teach in a dialogical way if we hope to open people not simply to the significance of other traditions but also to an understanding of differences. In most cases, this entails a radical revision of our pedagogy, one characterized less by providing persons with givens and more by opening possibilities for them to pursue their own questions, needs, and purposes.[113] Further, the dialogical relation, Nicholas Burbules observes, depends on sensitivity to the emotions involved—concern, trust, respect, appreciation, affection, hope—and on the fostering of "communicative virtues":

> They include such qualities as tolerance, patience, an openness to give and receive criticism, the inclination to admit that one may be mistaken, the desire to reinterpret or translate one's own concerns in a way that makes them comprehensible to others, the self-imposition of restraint in order that others may have a turn to speak, and—often neglected as a key element in dialogue—the willingness and ability to listen thoughtfully and attentively.[114]

An education for paradox depends upon the exercise of such virtues, just as interreligious encounter requires the virtues of spiritual regret and holy envy. If we are to stimulate religious commitments that are both clear and ambiguous, rooted and adaptive, then our task transcends the development of curricula and resources. We must nourish our own commitments as Christians by encounter with the "other" and embody in our teaching those virtues that will enable us to understand our faith more clearly because we understand it differently.

A final note. Some years ago I discovered this wry and perceptive observation on Christian liturgy by Annie Dillard:

> Why do we people in churches seem like cheerful, brainless tourists on a packaged tour of the Absolute?...On the whole, I do not find Christians, outside the catacombs, sufficiently sensible of conditions. Does anyone have the foggiest idea what sort of power we so blithely invoke? Or, as I suspect, does no one believe a word of it? The churches are children playing on the floor with their chemistry sets, mixing up a batch of TNT to kill a Sunday morning. It is madness to wear ladies' straw hats and velvet hats to church; we should all be wearing crash helmets. Ushers should issue life preserves and signal flares; they should lash us to our pews.[115]

As a Christian prone to be insufficiently "sensible of conditions," I am deeply grateful for the witness of peoples of other religious traditions, particularly Jews. Though I haven't yet brought my crash helmet to church, I've become acutely conscious of the depths to which the Divine Presence, manifest in so many mysterious ways, summons us Christians. And when I'm ready for my crash helmet, I suspect Sister Madeleva, no stranger herself to the ineffability and boundlessness of God, would gladly lend me hers.

1. See Sister M. Madeleva, C.S.C., *My First Seventy Years* (New York: Macmillan, 1959). See also the 1994 Madeleva lecture by Gail Porter Mandell, *Madeleva: One Woman's Life* (Mahwah, N.J.: Paulist Press, 1994).

2. Stephen L. Carter, *The Culture of Disbelief* (New York: Basic Books, 1993), pp. 36–37, 42.

3. David Tracy, *Plurality and Ambiguity: Hermeneutics, Religion and Hope* (San Francisco: Harper & Row, 1987), p. 85.

4. See Mary C. Boys, Sara S. Lee, and Dorothy C. Bass, "Protestant, Catholic, Jew: The Transformative Possibilities of Educating Across Religious Boundaries," *Religious Education* 90/2 (1995): 255–76.

5. I am following quite closely here an excerpt from John Coleman, "The Two Pedagogies: Discipleship and Citizenship," in Mary C. Boys, ed., *Education for Citizenship and Discipleship* (New York: Pilgrim Press, 1989), p. 45.

6. See Wade Clark Roof, *A Generation of Seekers: The Spiritual Journeys of the Baby Boom Generation* (San Francisco: HarperSan-Francisco, 1994).

7. Stephen Brookfield, *Developing Critical Thinkers* (San Francisco: Jossey-Bass, 1987), p. 46. "Premature ultimates" are "statements

uttered with such finality and conviction that the possibility of counterarguments is severely reduced....[They are] uncritical affirmations pretending to be reasoned arguments."

8. See Ralph Blumenthal, "The Maddening Mysteries of the Greatest Art Theft Ever," *New York Times,* December 15, 1994, sec. C, pp. 11, 14.

9. Cited in Rodger Kamenetz, *The Jew in the Lotus* (San Francisco: HarperSanFrancisco, 1994), p. 2.

10. Kamenetz, p. 92.

11. Irving Greenberg, *The Jewish Way* (New York: Summit Books, 1988), p. 287. See also Joseph Telushkin, *Jewish Literacy* (New York: Morrow, 1991).

12. Greenberg, p. 287.

13. Greenberg, p. 296.

14. Cited in Kamenetz, p. 107.

15. Kamenetz, p. 99.

16. Kamenetz, p. 230.

17. Kamentez, p. 188.

18. Kamenetz, p. 227.

19. Kamenetz, p. 192.

20. Kamenetz, p. 57.

21. Kamenetz, p. 283.

22. George Dardess, "When a Christian Chants the Qur'an," *Commonweal* 122/1 (January 13, 1995): 11–16.

23. Dardess, p. 13.

24. Dardess, p. 14.
25. Dardess, p. 14.
26. Dardess, p. 16.
27. Dardess, p. 16.
28. Dardess, p. 16.
29. Diana L. Eck, *Encountering God: A Spiritual Journey from Bozeman to Banaras* (Boston: Beacon, 1993).
30. Eck, p. xii.
31. Eck, p. 53.
32. Eck, p. 97.
33. Eck., p. 77.
34. Eck, p. 79.
35. Eck, p. 79.
36. Eck, p. 79.
37. Eck, p. 105.
38. Eck, p. 104.
39. Eck, p. 138.
40. Eck, pp. 140–41.
41. Eck, p. 142.
42. Eck, p. 163.
43. It is those whose primary focus is on the exoteric forms of religions who are most at risk, Katherine Kurs clarifies (personal communication to author, October 10, 1996).
44. Cited in Eck, pp. 164–65.
45. For a detailed account, see my article, "The Sisters of Sion: From a Conversionist Stance to a Dialogical Way of Life," *Journal of Ecumenical Studies* 31/1–2 (1994): 27–48. Quotations from

Sisters of Sion in this section are taken from the survey and interviews I did in researching the article.

46. Supersessionism (from the Latin, *supersedere,* to sit upon, to preside over) is the concept deeply embedded in Christian theology that Christians have replaced the Jews as God's people because the Jews rejected Jesus. By replacing the Jews, the church has thereby rendered Judaism obsolete.

47. Sr. Marie Carmelle, *Correspondence and Documents,* 1840–1853 (Rome: Tipografia Pontificia Universidad Gregoriana, 1979), p. 71.

48. Sr. Marie Carmelle, p. 305.

49 In 1949 Pope Pius XII ordered that the phrase "[pro] perfidis Judaeis" be translated into the vernacular as "unbelieving" rather than "perfidious" Jews—a half measure, at best.

50. See *Nostra Aetate* ("Declaration on the Relationship of the Church to Non-Christian Religions"), no. 4. *Nostra Aetate,* although a relatively modest statement in itself, opened a new era in relations between Catholics and Jews. A number of more detailed and forceful statements have subsequently been promulgated.

51. *Religious Education* 91/4 (1996). The theme of this issue is "Religious Traditions in Conversation;" it contains essays by eighteen

authors in addition to our own and an annotated bibliography on Jewish-Christian relations. Much of this section is drawn from the work jointly authored with Sara Lee or from conversations with her. All further references to articles in *Religious Education* are taken from the issue cited here.

52. See my essay, "A More Faithful Portrait of Judaism: An Imperative for Christian Educators," in David Efroymoson, Eugene Fisher, and Leon Klenicki, eds., *Within Context: Essays on Jews and Judaism in the New Testament* (Collegeville: The Liturgical Press, 1993), pp. 1–20.

53. Julie A. Collins, "Can I Not Do You as This Potter Has Done?" *Religious Education,* p. 468. For extensive documentation of changes among participants, see in the same issue Joanne Chafe, "Colloquium Participants Speak" (pp. 502–11), as well as the Boys and Lee essay, "The Catholic-Jewish Colloquium: An Experiment in Interreligious Learning" (pp. 421–66).

54. See Robert Tornberg, "On Finding More Pieces to the Puzzle," *Religious Education,* p. 498; and Cynthia Reich, "On Pluralism and Religious Education," *Religious Education,* p. 555.

55. David Ellenson, "Interreligious Learning and the Formation of Jewish Religious Identity," *Religious Education,* pp. 485–86.

56. Tornberg, p. 499.

57. Boys and Lee, p. 434.

58. Shira Lander and Daniel Lehmann, "New Wine for New Wineskins," *Religious Education,* p. 527.

59. Shulamith Reich Elster, "Learning with the Other," *Religious Education,* p. 569.

60. Ellenson, p. 487.

61. Collins, p. 469.

62. Sandra B. Lubarsky, "Dialogue: Holy Insecurity," *Religious Education,* p. 543.

63. Cited in Boys and Lee, p. 438.

64. Barbara Veale Smith, "Encountering the Other and Deepening in Faith," *Religious Education,* p. 564.

65. Lubarsky, p. 545.

66. John S. Dunne, *The Way of All the Earth* (New York: Macmillan, 1972), p. ix.

67. Darrell J. Fasching, *The Coming of the Millennium* (Valley Forge: Trinity Press International, 1996), p. 37.

68. Dwayne E. Huebner, "Educational Foundations for Dialogue," *Religious Education,* p. 585.

69. Huebner, p. 584.

70. Cited in Kamenetz, p. 49.

71. Eck, p. 193.

72. Eck, pp. 194–98.
73. Thomas Green, cited in James Wiggins, *In Praise of Religious Diversity* (New York: Routledge, 1996), p. 95.
74. Lee H. Yearley, *New Religious Virtues and the Study of Religion* (Tempe: Arizona State University, 1994), p. 12.
75. Boys and Lee, p. 444.
76. Yearley, p. 13.
77. Eck, p. 85.
78. Tornberg, p. 498.
79. Kamenetz, p. 280.
80. Kamenetz, p. 279.
81. See John C. Merkle, ed., *Abraham Joshua Heschel: Exploring His Life and Thought* (New York: Macmillan, 1985).
82. French Bishops' Committee for Relations with Jews, 1973, cited in Helga Croner, ed., *Stepping Stones to Further Jewish-Christian Relations* (New York: Stimulus Books, 1977), p. 61.
83. Clark Williamson, *A Guest in the House of Israel* (Louisville: Westminster/John Knox, 1993), p. 9.
84. Edward H. Flannery, *The Anguish of the Jews,* rev. and enlarged (Ramsey, N.J.: Paulist Press, 1985), p. 293.
85. See *The Jewish Way.*
86. Abraham Joshua Heschel, *The Sabbath: Its Meaning for Modern Man* (New York: Farrar, Straus and Giroux, 1951), p. 13. I have

changed the text to make his language inclusive of women.

87. Luke Timothy Johnson, *Faith's Freedom* (Minneapolis: Fortress, 1990), p. 65.

88. Dorothy C. Bass, "Keeping Sabbath," in D. Bass, ed., *Practicing Our Faith: A Way of Life for a Searching People* (San Francisco: Jossey-Bass, 1997), p. 86.

89. See John C. Merkle, "The Challenge of Jewish Spirituality to Christian Faith," in Arthur E. Zannoni, ed., *Proceedings of the Center for Jewish-Christian Learning* 6 (1991): 32–37.

90. *Gates of Prayer for Weekdays* (New York: Central Conference of American Rabbis, 1975), p. 36.

91. In Marge Piercy, *Available Light* (New York: Alfred Knopf), p. 123. For details of this prayer in Jewish liturgy, see Macy Nulman, *The Encyclopedia of Jewish Prayer* (Northvale, N.J.: Jason Aronson, 1993), pp. 255–56.

92. See Carol Ochs, *Women and Spirituality* (Notre Dame: University of Notre Dame Press, 1983) and *Song of the Self* (Philadelphia: Trinity Press International, 1994); Daniel Gordis, *God Was Not in the Fire: The Search for a Spiritual Judaism* (New York: Scribner's, 1995); and David J. Wolpe, *In Speech and in Silence* (New York: Henry Holt, 1992).

93. Everett Fox, *The Five Books of Moses: A New Translation with Introductions, Commentary and*

Notes (New York: Schocken Books, 1995), p. xxix and p. 273.

94. See Maurice Friedman, *Martin Buber: The Life of Dialogue* 3d ed. (Chicago: University of Chicago Press, 1976). I am indebted to Sandra Lubarsky for this reference.

95. I think not only of the corpus of the writings of Elie Wiesel, but also of David R. Blumenthal, *Facing the Abusing God: A Theology of Protest* (Louisville: Westminster/John Knox, 1993).

96. See Anson Laytner, *Arguing with God: A Jewish Tradition* (Northvale, N.J.: Jason Aronson, 1990).

97. I have found especially illuminating Gerd Theissen, *The Shadow of the Galilean* (Philadelphia: Fortress, 1987).

98. Daniel J. Harrington, "The Jewishness of Jesus: Facing Some Problems," in James Charlesworth, ed., *Jesus' Jewishness* (Philadelphia: The American Interfaith Institute; New York: Crossroad, 1991), p. 130.

99. The prayer is taken from the Rite of Acceptance into the Order of Catechumens. I have written about the symbol of the cross in "The Cross: Should a Symbol Betrayed Be Reclaimed?" *Cross Currents* 44/1 (1994): 5–27, and in "Jesus Through the Ages: Perspectives from the Cross," in Mary Christine Athans, ed., *Proceedings of the Center for Jewish-Christian Learning* 10 (1995): 13–22.

100. Roberta Bondi, *In Ordinary Time* (Nashville: Abingdon, 1995), p. 22.

101. Moving beyond parochial attitudes and convictions can be painful both on the personal and on the institutional level. As I worked on this text, for example, the *New York Times* carried a front-page story ("Can Non-Believers Be Saved?" August 22, 1996) about a serious conflict in the Reformed Church in American concerning the salvation of "non-Christians" (an unhappy term!). An experienced pastor of a large congregation in Michigan, Rev. Richard A. Rhem, had expressed his conviction that faith in Christ is not the sole means of salvation. "I believe the scope of God's grace is beyond the Christian community," said Rhem. In response, the regional church authority censured him in July, judging him in "disrepute before Christ, the church and the world."

102. This account is of my own composition, but it reflects what many, if not most, Christians learned about Christian origins.

103. For a summary, see my essay "A More Faithful Portrait of Judaism: An Imperative for Christian Educators," pp. 1–20. For an overview of the literature, see Mary C. Boys and Barbara Veale Smith, "Annotated Bibliography on Jewish-Christian Relations," *Religious Education,* pp. 601–19.

104. For a sampling of literature on these topics, see James Charlesworth et al., eds., *The Messiah: Developments in Earliest Judaism and Christianity* (Minneapolis: Augsburg Fortress, 1992); Anthony J. Saldarini, *Pharisees, Scribes and Sadducees* (Wilmington: Michael Glazier, 1988); Raymond E. Brown, *The Death of the Messiah*, 2 vols. (New York: Doubleday, 1994); and James D. G. Dunn, *The Partings of the Ways between Christianity and Judaism and Their Significance for the Character of Christianity* (London: SCM; Philadelphia: Trinity Press International, 1991).

105. See Katharine von Kellenbach, *Anti-Judaism in Feminist Religious Writings* (Atlanta: Scholars Press, 1994).

106. See the two collections of documents collected by Helga Croner, ed., *Stepping Stones to Further Jewish-Christian Relations* and *More Stepping Stones to Jewish-Christian Relations* (Mahwah, N.J.: Paulist Press, A Stimulus Book, 1985). The recent *Catechism of the Catholic Church,* however, is a supersessionist document in my judgment; see my "How Shall We Understand Jews and Judaism? Questions about the New Catechism," *Theology Today* 53/2 (1996): 165–70.

107. See Philip A. Cunningham, *Education for Shalom: Religion Textbooks and the Enhancement of the Catholic and Jewish Relationship*

(Collegeville: The Liturgical Press, 1994). Cf. Stuart Polly, *The Portrayal of Jews and Judaism in Current Protestant Teaching Materials* (Ann Arbor: University Microfilms International, 1992).

108. See Ellenson, pp. 480–88.

109. See Luke Timothy Johnson, "The New Testament's Anti-Jewish Slander and the Conventions of Ancient Polemic," *Journal of Biblical Literature* 108/3 (1989): 419–41.

110. Among the abundant literature, see Craig A. Evans and Donald A. Hagner, eds., *Anti-Semitism and Early Christianity* (Minneapolis: Fortress, 1993); Robert L. Wilken, *Judaism and the Early Christian Mind* (New Haven and London: Yale University Press, 1971) and idem, *John Chrysostom and the Jews* (Berkeley: University of California Press, 1983); and Robert S. MacLennan, *Early Christian Texts on Jews and Judaism* (Atlanta: Scholars Press, 1990).

111. "Notes on the Correct Way to Present Jews and Judaism in Preaching and Catechesis in the Roman Catholic Church," in *More Stepping Stones to Jewish-Christian Relations,* no. 27, pp. 231–32.

112. Fasching, p. 70.

113. See Nicholas C. Burbules, *Dialogue in Teaching: Theory and Practice* (New York: Teachers College Press, 1993), p. 10.
114. Barbules, p. 42.
115. Annie Dillard, *Teaching a Stone to Talk* (New York: HarperCollins, 1982), p. 58.

The Madeleva Lecture in Spirituality

This series, sponsored by the Center for Spirituality, Saint Mary's College, Notre Dame, Indiana, honors annually the woman who as president of the college inaugurated its pioneering graduate program in theology, Sister M. Madeleva, C.S.C.

1985
Monika K. Hellwig
Christian Women in a Troubled World

1986
Sandra M. Schneiders
Women and the Word

1987
Mary Collins
Women at Prayer

1988
Maria Harris
Women and Teaching

1989
Elizabeth Dreyer
Passionate Women: Two Medieval Mystics

1990
Joan Chittister
Job's Daughters

1991
Dolores R. Leckey
Women and Creativity

1992
Lisa Sowle Cahill
Women and Sexuality

1993
Elizabeth A. Johnson
Women, Earth and Creator Spirit

1994
Gail Porter Mandell
Madeleva: One Woman's Life

1995
Diana L. Hayes
Hagar's Daughters

1996
Jean Rodriguez
Stories We Live:
Cuentos Que Vivimos